The Lean CFO

This book is not about debits, credits, or accounting theory. It's about how a chief financial officer (CFO) becomes a Lean CFO to lead the transformation of a company's management accounting system into a lean management accounting system.

It's been well established in lean companies that traditional management accounting systems do not provide relevant and reliable information to decision makers. The CFO, as steward of a company's management accounting system, must provide the leadership to improve the quality of the information produced by a company's management accounting system so it is aligned with a company's lean strategy, lean operations, and continuous improvement.

The integration of a lean management accounting system with a company's lean strategy will lead to improved decision making by all users and drive long-term financial success. Lean management accounting helps all users, from executives to line managers, better understand the relationships between lean operating performance and financial performance.

Written in the style of a practice guide, *The Lean CFO* is written not just for CFOs, but for all stakeholders of a company's management accounting system, such as executives and owners, lean leaders, functional managers, and accounting professionals.

The Lean CFO

Architect of the Lean Management Accounting System

Second Edition

Nicholas S. Katko

Routledge
Taylor & Francis Group

NEW YORK AND LONDON

First published 2023
by Routledge
605 Third Avenue, New York, NY 10158

and by Routledge
4 Park Square, Milton Park, Abingdon, Oxon, OX14 4RN

Routledge is an imprint of the Taylor & Francis Group, an informa business

ISBN: 978-1-032-30241-6 (hbk)
ISBN: 978-1-032-30239-3 (pbk)
ISBN: 978-1-003-30409-8 (ebk)

DOI: 10.4324/9781003304098

Typeset in Minion
by Newgen Publishing UK

Printed in the United Kingdom
by Henry Ling Limited

Contents

Preface to the Second Edition

As I was writing *Practicing Lean Accounting* with Mike De Luca, I often referred back to the first edition of *The Lean CFO*. What I recognized when I re-read it is that how I think about, teach, and explain lean management accounting has changed since the first edition was published.

So, in the spirit of continuous improvement, I decided to write a second edition. The layout of the second edition now follows a lean management accounting transformation process. The entire book has been re-written to be industry neutral, rather than manufacturing centric. Another objective in re-writing was to better explain how lean management accounting and lean practices work together to create a lean management accounting system.

I'd like to thank the following people for their help and support in writing this book:

- Deanna Katko – for supporting me all the way and encouraging me.
- Karyn Ross – for her editing of the book.
- Michael Sinocchi and Samantha Dalton of Taylor & Francis for agreeing to publish a second edition.
- Every company I have ever worked with – working with you allowed me to improve my approach to teaching and consulting on lean management accounting.

I hope you enjoy reading the book and best wishes on your lean management accounting transformation!

About the Author

Nicholas S. Katko's 30-year lean accounting career began in the 1990s at Bullard, where as CFO he implemented a complete lean accounting system in conjunction with Bullard's lean transformation. After Bullard, Nick and his wife Deanna started Strategic Financial Solutions, Inc. which provides bookkeeping and tax services (Deanna's area of expertise) and lean accounting-based contract CFO services (Nick's area of expertise) to companies in the Lexington, Kentucky region.

Simultaneously, Nick began working with Brian Maskell at BMA (www.maskell.com) as a senior consultant providing lean accounting training, coaching and consulting to companies of all industries worldwide. Upon Brian's retirement in 2018, Nick became owner and President of BMA.

Nick is a regular speaker at the annual Lean Accounting Summit and has also presented at conferences in the United States, Europe, Asia and Australia.

Nick is the co-author of *Practicing Lean Accounting* (2021); author of *The Lean CFO* (2013), which has been translated into Turkish, Italian and Russian; and co-author of *The Lean Business Management System* (2007). Nick's periodic articles on lean accounting have appeared in *The Journal of Cost Management* and other publications.

Nick is a Certified Public Accountant, and has a BS in Accounting and an MBA in Finance, both from the University of Kentucky. Nick lives in Lexington, Kentucky with his wife Deanna and their family.

Nick Katko
nkatko@maskell.com
www.maskell.com

1

The Lean Management Accounting System

If you do an internet search for the definition of lean management accounting, you will get many results, but most try to explain it in this way:

> Management accounting is providing financial and non-financial information to managers for them to use to make decisions.

When defined this narrowly, it sounds like something that is just in the accounting function. But if management accounting is viewed as a system, as illustrated in Figure 1.1, accounting is only a small part. The management accounting system consists of a vast database of financial and non-financial information in various systems that record, store and synthesize the information. It consists of every user of the information, from senior leaders all the way down to line managers. It consists of all the analytical and decision-making practices all these users perform. Accounting is the steward of the system; it is also a user, and it is an analytical service provider to other users.

When a company commits to a lean strategy, all processes, systems, people, actions and information in the company must be aligned to the strategy to ensure success. This means a company's management accounting system must become its *lean* management accounting system.

This is a transformation process, and this book is written to explain that process. Figure 1.2 illustrates the basic architecture of a lean management accounting system and is also how this book is laid out:

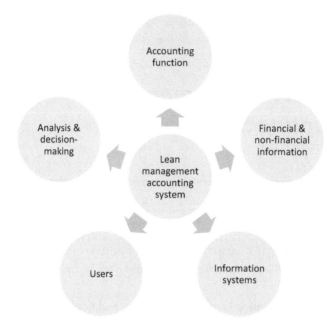

FIGURE 1.1
Management Accounting System

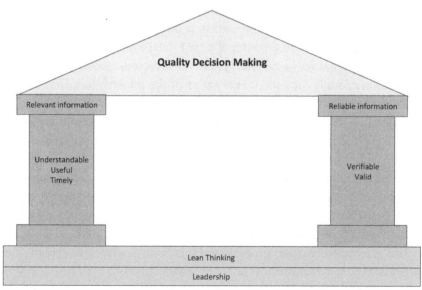

FIGURE 1.2
Architecture of a Lean Management Accounting System

- **Chapter 2: Leading a Lean Accounting Transformation** – for a lean management accounting transformation to be successful, it is essential that the CFO become a Lean CFO to lead the transformation. This chapter will explain the qualities and characteristics of a Lean CFO and provide effective strategies to ensure a successful transformation.
- **Chapter 3: Lean Is the Strategy** – a lean management accounting system rests on the foundation of lean principles, practices and tools. It must also support how lean works to create financial improvement. This chapter summarizes the relationships between lean and a lean management accounting system.
- **Chapters 4, 5 and 6: The Box Score – Relevant and Reliable Information** – these chapters explain the relevant and reliable financial and non-financial information needed in a lean management accounting system. Chapter 4 explains how to build a lean performance measurement system. Chapter 5 explains how to calculate and measure capacity. Chapter 6 explains how to build value stream income statements. This relevant and reliable information is presented as value stream box scores, as illustrated in Figure 1.3.
- **Chapters 7 and 8: Quality Decision Making** – these chapters explain how box scores and the components of box scores are used to align analysis and decision making from senior leadership to line managers. Chapter 7 explains how box scores are integrated with lean practices to create a value stream management system to plan, improve, control and manage value streams. Chapter 8 explains how to incorporate box scores into analysis and decision making as it relates to understanding the profitability of decisions.
- **Chapters 9, 10 and 11: Dealing with Standard Costing** – in many manufacturing companies, and some non-manufacturing companies, standard costing systems are deeply integrated in management accounting systems. Because it has been shown for over 30 years that standard costing information doesn't provide relevant and reliable information in lean companies, it is essential to develop a plan to separate standard costing from a lean management accounting system. Chapter 9 explains how to eliminate waste in standard costing systems. Chapter 10 explains how to eliminate waste in ERP transaction processing. Chapter 11 explains how to "turn off standard costing" for inventory valuation purposes.

	Current State	Future State
Performance Measurements		
Productivity	$ 27,797	$ 34,490
Delivery	81%	100%
Cost	$ 207	$ 145
Quality	84.6%	92.2%
Days Inventory	29.25	29.25
Average Lead Time	10.78	8.62
Capacity		
Productive	33.51%	36.38%
Nonproductive	45.73%	35.39%
Available	14.71%	22.18%
Income Statement		
Revenue	861,696	1,069,200
Materials	292,516	234,013
Contribution Margin	569,180	835,187
Direct Costs	127,484	127,583
Shared Costs	29,527	29,528
Total Production Costs	157,011	157,111
Value Stream Operating Profit	412,169	678,077
	47.8%	63.4%

FIGURE 1.3
The Box Score

- **Appendix: Lean Management Accounting Transformation Checklists** – these checklists have been designed to help plan and manage your lean management accounting transformation. These checklists are also available online at www.maskell.com.

Now it's time to build your company's lean management accounting system.

2

Leading a Lean Management Accounting Transformation

My first exposure to lean was as CFO at Bullard. As a management team, before we began our lean transformation, we read *The Machine That Changed the World*. What I got out of the book was that lean was something "done" in manufacturing operations, and it made sense to me.

We hired a vice president of manufacturing with lean experience, and he immediately began developing a relationship with me regarding how I, and accounting, could help the transformation by providing better financial and non-financial information. He also made sure to include me in operational meetings where lean plans were discussed and went out of his way to explain the "whys" of the plan.

Little did I know, he was working on teaching me about lean and helping me adopt a different mindset about what lean is. He was coaching me on the importance of accounting providing operations the right information. He was helping me become a *Lean* CFO, which I figured out when I began connecting the operational improvements made to Bullard's improved financial performance. After I made these connections, I was "all in" on lean. I became a lean leader within the company and began thinking of myself as a Lean CFO.

Over the years in working with many companies, I have seen other CFOs (and controllers, cost accountants, accounting managers and analysts) go through the same transformation, where they mentally now put "lean" as the first word in their job title. I've also seen others adopt a "wait and see" approach – it makes sense to them, but they want to "see" something (what they want to see is usually vague) before committing. A "wait and see" approach does not work for accounting leaders in a lean transformation.

DOI: 10.4324/9781003304098-2   5

In lean companies, it's essential that the CFO become a *Lean* CFO early in the lean management accounting transformation process because *you must be the leader.* In smaller companies you may be actively involved in transformation activities. In larger companies, you probably will delegate the detail work to others in accounting, but ultimately you are leading them.

What I'm going to explain next are the behaviors a Lean CFO needs to lead the transformation as well as broad methods the Lean CFO can use to enable the success of the transformation.

BECOME THE ROLE MODEL

Successful leaders are role models, genuinely practicing the thinking, behaviors, and characteristics they want those they lead to emulate. As a senior leader in the company, a CFO's words, actions and behavior are watched by everyone. Those watching can spot a fake miles away, so it's important that the Lean CFO's beliefs and behaviors are genuine. Here is a summary of what you need to do:

- Change your thinking – you must believe in the benefits of lean management accounting before you begin a transformation. It's important to understand how lean can drive financial improvement over time. As a leader, it is important to communicate a clear vision and/or goals regarding lean management accounting and how it will benefit the company.
- You will learn with everyone else – a lean management accounting transformation is really a long-term learning experience for you, for accounting and for all users of management accounting information. When others see you learning, they will open their minds to learning.
- Show you care about people – show that you care about people as they go through the process of learning how to use a lean management accounting system. There will be those who "get it" quickly and others that may take more time learning. Help everyone work through the learning process. Be a coach by asking, listening, engaging and influencing others in a positive way.
- Don't let interruptions get in the way – I've seen some companies and CFOs put a pause on a lean management accounting transformation

for "business reasons" that from my viewpoint appear to be a normal part of running a business, rather than extraordinary economic events. Pausing the transformation tells everyone lean management accounting is not that important.

INTEGRATE LEAN MANAGEMENT ACCOUNTING INTO THE LEAN STRATEGY

Senior leaders of the company must give unequivocal and unwavering support to developing and using a lean management accounting system. Senior leaders must make lean management accounting an essential part of a company's overall lean strategy. As with any component of a strategy, lean management accounting must have an action plan to develop and deploy over time. If it is not part of the company's lean strategy, a transformation will not be successful. As a Lean CFO, and member of the senior leadership team, you must work to make this happen.

Lean management accounting is a company commitment because of the many users of the information and analytical services a management accounting system provides. These users are in every function in a company, and they are the customers of the lean management accounting system. As customers, they define the quality standards for the information and analytical practices in a lean management accounting system. For these reasons it is important to include users in the lean management accounting transformation.

USE LEAN PRACTICES AS THE FOUNDATION FOR THE TRANSFORMATION

A lean management accounting transformation is not like a project with a definitive end. It is just like a lean transformation, which begins and really never ends because there are always opportunities to improve and serve customers better.

The format and content of this book are laid out as a general roadmap of how to execute a lean management accounting transformation. In the book I'll explain the numbers of lean management accounting and how they are integrated with lean practices and used in analysis and decision making. What I am going to explain here is how to apply some specific lean concepts and practices to the transformation process to enable success.

Customer Value

As you will read in the next chapter, customer value is the first principle of lean. It is really the overarching purpose of lean – to serve customers better. The same holds true for lean management accounting. It needs to serve its customers (users of information) better by providing them useful, understandable, relevant and timely information and analytical practices that are aligned with lean. This needs to be clearly understood by both accounting, the supplier of products and services, and its customers, the users.

Continuous Improvement

A difference between conventional management accounting systems and lean management accounting is that lean companies will strive to continuously improve their systems for two reasons. The first is that improvement may be required to meet the changing needs of its customers. The second is that companies must also strive to continually eliminate waste in lean management accounting systems. Those wastes are summarized in Figure 2.1.

Defects	• information not useful to users
Overproduction	• reports not used by users
Waiting	• users waiting for information
Neglect of talent	• accounting performing work below their skill level
Transportation	• handoffs of information between systems
Inventory	• batch processing of information
Motion	• meetings to understand information
Excess processing	• unnecessary transactions, reporting and analyses

FIGURE 2.1
Management Accounting System Waste

Defects	• product costs, variances and absorption
Overproduction	• reports produced and ignored by operations
Waiting	• users waiting for information that is not timely
Neglect of talent	• accounting processing information instead of analyzing
Transportation	• information handoffs – systems, spreadsheets, reports
Inventory	• monthly reporting; annual rate setting
Motion	• meetings and communication to explain numbers
Excess processing	• shop floor reporting, time tracking, detailed rate setting

FIGURE 2.2
Examples of Waste in Manufacturing Management Accounting

Waste exists in every process, in every company. It is a matter of making the waste visible in order to improve. Figure 2.2 expands on Figure 2.1 by illustrating the actual types of waste which are typically present in manufacturing management accounting systems. As will be explained in the next chapter, eliminating waste creates capacity, or, in other words, more time, which can be applied to more value added activities. In lean management accounting this means accounting can spend more time on value added analysis and those who report information into systems can be freed up and reassigned to value added work.

Continuous improvement also forms the foundation of the lean management accounting transformation process and is effective in changing "project-based" thinking. Breaking down what sounds to others like a massive project into smaller improvement events makes it easier for everyone to grasp.

Figure 2.3 illustrates the typical steps in a lean management accounting transformation process. In the beginning of a transformation, an initial future state for each step must be completed before moving on to the next step. For each step, further improvement opportunities are identified, and subsequent future states are created. Ask anyone at a company where lean management accounting has been in place for a number of years, and they will tell you how much their system has evolved over time.

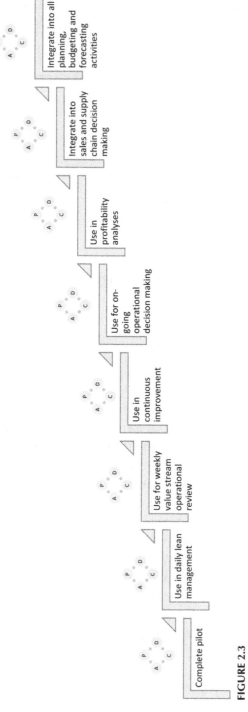

FIGURE 2.3

Continuous Improvement Cycles for Lean Accounting

Use PDCA

It is inevitable that a lean management accounting transformation will encounter problems, issues and obstacles. Some of these may be known up front and others may arise during the transformation process. Using PDCA (Plan-Do-Check-Adjust) is the proven lean method for solving problems.

Lean companies use PDCA as the framework for teaching employees how to solve problems and for all improvement activities. It is equally applicable to all issues encountered in the lean management accounting transformation process. Using PDCA will get to the root cause of the problem, and once the actual root cause is known, solutions can be put in place to eliminate, or reduce the effect of, the root cause.

Focus on Thinking

Users process the information from management accounting systems in their analytical and decision-making activities. They think using the information, draw conclusions and recommend actions. In a lean management accounting transformation, there will be some new numbers to use in existing analytical practices, some new analytical practices, and some analytical practices which may need to stop.

All this change may be very difficult for some decision makers, and their reactions may appear to indicate they are resisting or pushing back on the changes. Don't make those assumptions. Assume they need more time to practice and learn new thinking habits, and provide coaching for them to facilitate the learning process.

The best people to serve as coaches to users are those in finance and accounting who have the most interaction with the users, such as controllers, cost accountants and analysts. These accounting team members should be developed into "lean accountants" early in the lean management accounting transformation. How should this be done? Using the same process you use to become a Lean CFO!

There are other benefits of developing lean accounting coaches. One benefit is breaking down the artificial functional barriers and developing stronger relationships between accounting and other functions. The other benefit is that lean accounting coaches learn more about how lean practices are being applied in the company, and begin making connections to financial performance.

Start with Pilots

Lean transformations begin with pilots, such as taking one linear production cell, turning it into a U-shaped cell and creating single piece flow through the cell. This is done so the team can actually experience lean practices and others can see how lean practices work. Lean pilots demonstrate the benefits of lean physical flow.

Piloting lean management accounting in analysis and decision making does the same, it proves the benefits of improving the quality of decision making. When I work with companies on their lean management accounting transformations, the first step is to pilot lean management accounting in one value stream, by developing its box score and using the box score in some basic operating decision making.

Piloting lean management accounting in one value stream also can make visible problems or issues that must be dealt with in subsequent deployments to other value streams. The PDCA approach can adjust the deployment plan to mitigate these problems in other value streams.

The pilot team, with real life experience under their belt, can also serve as lean management accounting coaches. Because they have experienced the entire process, they are in a position to help others. This is invaluable as the transformation is expanded into all parts of the company.

WRAP UP: YOU ARE THE HEAD COACH

At the same time Bullard began its lean transformation, I was coaching our younger son's youth baseball team (ages 9–12). I quickly learned that as their coach they were watching my every move and reaction, whether in practice or during games. They were also listening to every word I said, and how I said it. The kids on the team were also at different levels of skills, experience and confidence. I realized I needed to coach each player individually, based on where they were in developing baseball skills, and I also needed to coach the team collectively in how to play as a team. It was also obvious to me that they could tell the difference between me being genuine and phony.

The most important lesson I learned from coaching the team was that it really was no different from being a CFO!

The accounting department was my "team" of players. I had to follow the same coaching practices with them that I used with the baseball team. Also, as a member of the senior management team, I had the same obligation to all the other employees in the company as I did with the accounting team. I stopped thinking of myself as a manager (and acting like one) and started thinking and acting like a coach.

The result? We were a close-knit team that embraced improving together. We developed strong relationships with each other. We truly enjoyed the time we spent together.

We won the youth league championship that year.

We started a successful lean management accounting transformation the same year.

You, and your company, can also "win" a lean management accounting transformation with leadership. Now let's dive into the details on how to make lean management accounting a reality.

3

Lean is the Strategy

INTRODUCTION

If an architect is going to design a new building, they must start with the foundation of the building. A poorly designed foundation will not be able to support the building. Applying this analogy to lean management accounting, the foundation that's needed is lean thinking.

Based on my experience, there are five aspects of lean that create the strong foundation for a lean management accounting system:

- Lean is the strategy
- The value stream organization
- People solving problems
- Lean operating practices
- The economics of lean

The relationships between each of these aspects of lean and a lean management accounting system need to be understood by a Lean CFO in planning and executing a lean management accounting transformation. What follows is a high level summary of each of these aspects rather than a detailed explanation of lean practices.

LEAN IS THE STRATEGY

To achieve financial success with lean, it must be *the* strategy of a company. Some companies understand this, but other companies think lean is a component of their strategy. This distinction may not seem that important, but it has a dramatic impact on what a company thinks it can accomplish operationally and financially with lean.

If a company thinks lean is "part" of a business strategy, then it usually selectively implements certain lean practices or rationalizes its current business practices as "being lean." In the lean community, this is known by the acronym LINO ("Lean in name only") and is a "tools-based" approach to lean. This approach usually leads to employees thinking of lean as what some people call "the flavor of the month" – just another initiative senior leaders are rolling out that will eventually go away, and the company will return to business as usual.

Another possible outcome of approaching lean in this manner is that lean is restarted multiple times. Selected lean practices are put into place but not sustained. Lean practices regress back to old non-lean practices. Then a few years later, the company tries to restart lean, and the same cycle repeats itself. To avoid these common pitfalls, it's best to think of lean as *the* strategy of the company.

Customer Value

Lean is a business strategy based on serving customers better. To actually serve customers better, a company must clearly understand value *from the customer's perspective*, and it must *actually deliver* the value the customers want. By doing both, a company will change the dynamics of its relationships with customers and its competition.

It's not difficult to determine what most customers want from companies they buy products and services from. Customers expect quality, as defined by the customer. Customers expect on-time delivery, based on when they want the product or service delivered. Customers also expect an overall satisfying experience in dealing with the company beyond quality and delivery.

Customer value is created every time a customer has an encounter with a company. Think of all the encounters your customers have with your company outside of the actual use of your product or service. Placing an order, receiving and paying the invoice, after-sales support, navigating your website and the ease of talking to a person in your company; these are just some examples of where value can be created. Lean companies understand these touch points between a company and its customers are all opportunities to serve customers better.

An effective lean management accounting system is one that focuses on servicing its customers (who happen to be internal users) better. What the customers of a lean management accounting system value is the same as what your external customers value from your company:

- Quality – useful and understandable information that is based on lean thinking rather than traditional business practices.
- Delivery – the useful and understandable information must be timely and available to users for the particular analysis or decision they are making.
- Service – accounting must provide value in decision support for internal users rather than being aloof, isolated or disengaged from lean.

A Lean Strategy is Principle-Based

What separates lean from other business strategies is that it is based on a few principles rather than specific goals that change year-to-year. If you would like to learn in detail about the principles of lean, I recommend finding one of many great lean books that are available. What I'm going to do here is to summarize them in a few paragraphs, then explain in more detail how lean principles also apply to lean management accounting.

Lean originated in Toyota as the Toyota Production System and its principal architect, Taiichi Ohno, articulated two basic principles: continuous improvement and respect for people. Continuous improvement focuses on long-term improvement rather than short-term gains. Respect for people is basically about listening to the employees who perform the work because they are closest to the real problems, and oftentimes have the best solutions to the problems.

The actual term "lean" was introduced by Jim Womack and Daniel Jones in the book *Lean Thinking*. In this book, they described five principles of lean to better explain how the Toyota Production System could apply to any business, not just an automotive manufacturer. The five principles they explained were: customer value, value streams, flow and pull, pursuing perfection, and empowering employees.

Because the principles of lean are consistent and don't change year-to-year like traditional strategic objectives, they force the leaders of companies to take a long-term view of a business.

Lean principles also serve as a "True North" to align all initiatives, actions and operating practices around a few basic principles. The purpose of lean practices, tools and methods is supported by the principles. Lean principles are very good at answering "why" questions such as:

- Why do we have to improve?
- Why do we need to understand waste?
- Why do we have to adopt lean practices such as kanban?

Lean principles should be used to develop a corresponding set of lean management accounting principles which can be used as a foundation to drive a lean management accounting transformation. Lean management accounting principles can be used to answer the "why does the current management accounting system have to change?" questions that will arise.

Figure 3.1 illustrates how to develop lean management accounting system principles based on the five principles of lean. *A lean management accounting system creates value for its customers by providing relevant and reliable information that is aligned to value streams.* The information needs to be available to users when it is needed. Accounting, as stewards of a lean

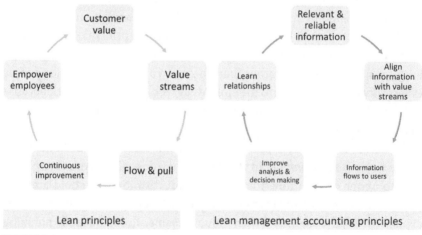

FIGURE 3.1
Examples of Lean Management Accounting Principles

management accounting system, focus on improving the analytical and decision-making practices of the company with quality information. The lean management accounting system is also a system designed for enabling learning, so users can learn the dynamic cause–effect relationships between lean operating performance and financial performance to drive long-term financial success.

Now let's look at the next aspect of lean, the value stream organization, and its impact on a lean management accounting system.

VALUE STREAM ORGANIZATION

In order to serve customers better, a lean company must gain insight and understanding as to exactly how it serves its customers, which are the value streams of a company. Figure 3.2 summarizes the definition of a value stream. A value stream is the sequence of process steps from the time a customer places an order to the time the customer receives the product or service, executed at the proper time. The process steps of a value stream flow horizontally through the traditional vertical, departmental organizational structure of a company.

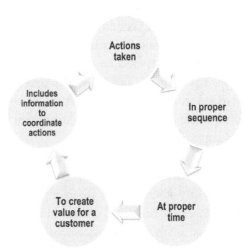

FIGURE 3.2
Definition of a Value Stream

The first step in creating a value stream organization is to identify a company's value streams. This is a logical, rational exercise that is conducted through direct observation from the time of receipt of a customer order to the shipment of the product or delivery of a service. This exercise is sometimes called "stapling yourself to an order."

Experience matters in the process of identifying value streams. It's best for someone who has done this before to facilitate the process to avoid common mistakes such as:

- Assuming that "we already know" our value streams intuitively.
- Identifying value streams by sitting around a table in a conference room.
- Top-down identification of value streams by senior leaders.
- A never-ending discussion about what a company's value streams are.

After value streams have been identified, the next step is to organize around the value streams. Lean companies focus on optimizing value stream operating performance rather than optimizing performance of vertical departments. Lean companies improve by value stream rather than random improvement by departments. Lean companies plan by value stream rather than by traditional top-down planning methods. This requires a level of value stream organization.

A common misperception when people hear "create a value stream organization" is that it means an organizational restructuring of the company, which is difficult to do. The common approach to creating the value stream organization is to develop a matrix organization where value stream teams have responsibility and accountability for horizontal flow: operational control, improvement and overall management of the value streams, as summarized in Figure 3.3. The vertical departments still exist more as "subject matter experts" providing value stream teams with technical standards and support.

Here is a simple example. In a traditional manufacturing company, the quality department performs quality inspections in operations as well as maintaining overall quality standards for the company. In a value stream organization, the quality department still sets and maintains overall quality standards, but the actual inspection activities are incorporated into the daily work of the employees in each value stream.

Organizational changes	Self-directed teams
• reduce or eliminate departments • change reporting relationships • *difficult to do initially, but possible*	• teams have responsibility and authority • dotted-line reporting to functional managers and leaders • *recommended approach*

FIGURE 3.3
Methods to Create a Value Stream Organization

A lean management accounting system is value stream centric. In order to optimize value stream performance, it must be measured. The relationships between value stream operating performance and financial performance must be clearly understood by everyone. Lean management accounting systems must transition away from traditional cost-based information, such as product costs or actual-to-budget reports, and provide the useful and understandable information for effective value stream management.

CONTINUOUS IMPROVEMENT = PEOPLE SOLVING PROBLEMS

Many companies claim they focus on improvement, but oftentimes this is more a traditional top-down approach where company leaders dictate initiatives. Many companies also consider firefighting a form of improvement. Lean companies take a different approach. Lean companies focus on people solving problems because they understand that the employees who do the work understand the root causes of problems the best.

In lean companies, improvement is not random, haphazard or dictated by top management. Lean companies use the scientific method as a framework for teaching employees how to solve problems. The application of the scientific method inside a lean company usually goes by the acronym PDCA (plan, do, check, adjust), A-3 Thinking or simply lean problem

No standard	• process has no standards of performance
Troubleshooting	• immediate responses to abnormal conditions
Gap from standard	• actual performance did not meet standard
Improve the standard	• create a new, improved standard of performance

FIGURE 3.4
Types of Problems

solving (in this book I'm going to use PDCA to describe lean problem solving).

The first step in the problem solving is to be able to properly identify a problem. Lean companies recognize that not all problems are created equal, and different types of problems require different responses. Figure 3.4 summarizes how most lean companies categorize problems. Let's take a look at each type of problem and typical responses.

No Standard

Experienced lean practitioners understand that problems cannot be identified, and true continuous improvement cannot take place, if there is no standard of performance. Another way to think about this is "what should be happening." It is important to identify if this is the "current state" of a process because this problem needs to be solved first. Developing a standard of performance is about creating a level of stability in process performance to be able to begin troubleshooting and identify gaps from standards.

Troubleshooting

Lean companies recognize problems will occur and methods must exist to react to problems as they occur. Troubleshooting is simply having standard responses to abnormal conditions and is also known as short-term countermeasures. Effective troubleshooting is the opposite of traditional business firefighting. It requires the people who work in a process to recognize abnormal conditions as they arise and react in a standard, methodical fashion. Effective troubleshooting mitigates the impact of the problem on process performance.

The classic lean example of troubleshooting is the ability of an assembly line operator in Toyota to "stop the line" if an abnormal condition is identified. This creates an Andon (a signal) for a team of people to go to where the problem exists to troubleshoot and restart the assembly line.

Gap from Standard

Having performance standards in place allows for measuring actual performance against the standards. The objective of identifying gaps from standard is for a process team to understand the root causes of the gaps and make the necessary improvements to eliminate the gaps. One example is schedule attainment, where a process has a schedule of work to meet (the standard), such as completing specific orders for a day. If the schedule is not achieved, there is a gap from standard and the team's responsibility is to understand the root causes.

Improving the Standard

This is proactive problem solving – by planning and conducting structured improvement events to create a new improved standard of performance (the future state). This is what most people think when they hear "continuous improvement." The most common example is a multi-day kaizen event, where a team of people work on one specific problem, such as reducing the set-up time on a machine by 50% or reducing month-end close by three days.

A process problem can only be identified if process performance is measured. Process performance standards are numbers, such as on-time delivery, lead time or scrap rates. An effective lean management accounting system must provide process teams with timely performance measurements that allow them to identify each type of problem and measure the effectiveness of troubleshooting and improvements. The reporting of the performance measurements must match the speed at which a process must respond to problems.

LEAN OPERATING PRACTICES

Another characteristic of companies that have achieved successful lean transformations is they focus on integrating lean thinking into the fabric of everyday work through a variety of tools and methods, some of which are summarized in Figure 3.5. Another way to think of this is lean is practiced every day, everywhere, by everybody, all the time. This means the strategy is being executed on a daily basis.

Creating flow, at the pull of the customer, is probably the hardest part of becoming a truly lean company. Another way to explain this is that any process should be as fast as possible to meet the exact demand of the customer. This is difficult because establishing flow requires "system-thinking": the entire value stream needs to work in a coordinated manner to meet exact, specific customer needs and maintain productivity levels. This requires everyone working in a value stream to have a good understanding of customer needs – both the company's customers and also all downstream process steps in the value stream.

This difficulty is overcome by using value stream mapping. A current state map, as illustrated in Figure 3.6, makes visible what is preventing flow. A future state map, as illustrated in Figure 3.7, is how flow is created through the application of lean practices. Once flow is established, it must be measured by the process team so that interruptions to flow (gaps from standard) are quickly discovered and addressed.

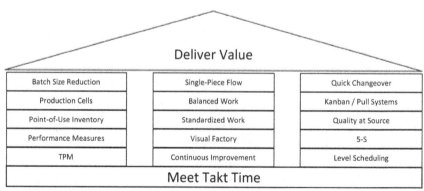

FIGURE 3.5
Lean Tools and Methods

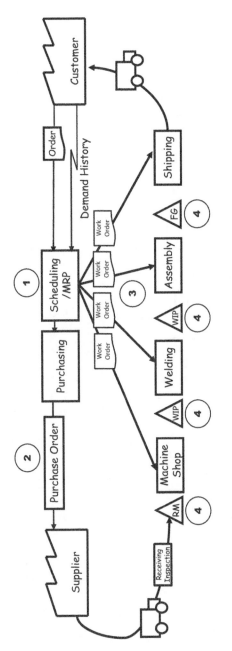

Traditional manufacturing PUSH methodology: each department executes its plan

1. Demand history and current orders are used by Scheduling & Planning to create the production plan
2. Purchasing receives a purchase forecast from MRP and is responsible for buying materials according to the plan
3. Each manufacturing department receives work orders from MRP and is responsible for executing the production plan
4. The result: Inventory

FIGURE 3.6

Current State Value Stream Map

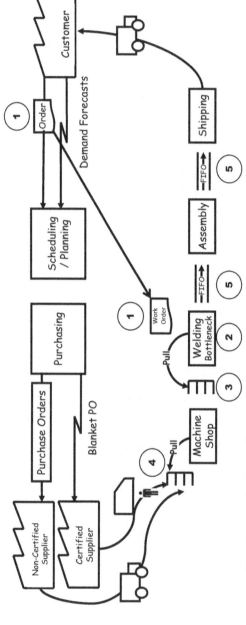

Flow is created with a pull system

1. Production is based on actual demand, not on an MRP-generated forecast.
2. Every value stream has a bottleneck – i.e. the process step with the longest cycle time – and this is the only step which needs to be scheduled. Welding is the bottleneck process in this value stream.
3. A supermarket is created between Machining and Welding to regulate the work of Machining, so it matches the rate of work in Welding. Machining will replenish this supermarket at the rate that Welding pulls.
4. A pull system is established between Machining and suppliers. Machining signals suppliers when its inventory needs to be replenished. The supplier delivers at regular intervals.
5. Because Assembly works faster than Welding, it produces one-at-a-time as Welding completes its work. Then the finished product flows directly to Shipping for delivery to the customer.

The result: Dramatic reduction of inventory.

FIGURE 3.7

Future State Value Stream Map

Traditional management accounting systems usually are aligned to the monthly financial reporting cycle and are designed primarily to analyze costs. Lean management accounting systems must be aligned with, and support, lean operating practices. This means it must deliver timely information to measure and manage flow. It must provide timely information for daily and weekly lean management cycles. Lean management accounting systems must also supply the relevant and reliable information for value stream mapping and improvement events.

THE ECONOMICS OF LEAN

Business strategies are designed to drive financial success, and lean is no different. What is different with a lean business strategy is that financial improvement is a long-term outcome of serving customers better and eliminating waste through continuous improvement. It takes time for employees to learn how to solve problems and conduct improvement events. It takes time to install and use all of the lean operational tools, practices and methods to improve flow. These are the reasons lean companies take a long-term view of financial improvement.

I call this the economics of lean, which is summarized in Figure 3.8. Continuous improvement eliminates waste, which creates capacity. In the short term, the creation of capacity does not have an immediate financial impact. It's how this newly created capacity is used that determines the financial impact.

Using capacity to serve customers better, such as by reducing lead times and improving delivery, has the potential to create a competitive advantage for a company. This can lead to sales growth above and beyond a company's historical growth rate. While CFO at Bullard I learned this firsthand. We were able to reduce order fulfillment lead time to three days (while reducing inventory) and achieve over 95% on-time delivery. By serving customers better than the competition, this increased our sales growth rate from single digits to double digits.

Using capacity to improve flow also generates productivity gains, which means a value stream can increase its output with the same or fewer resources. Improving productivity controls costs by achieving some actual

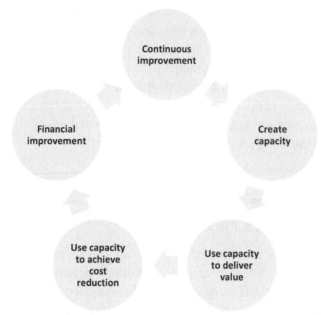

FIGURE 3.8
Economics of Lean

cost savings but more significantly by avoiding future cost increases, such as hiring more people or buying more machines.

A lean management accounting system's analytical and decision-making practices must be based on the economics of lean in order to realize the financial improvement that can result from continuous improvement.

WRAP UP – LEAN IS THE STRATEGY

The foundations for an effective lean management accounting system, leadership and lean thinking have now been built. The next step is to build the support structure, the numbers of a lean management accounting system, that will provide the relevant and reliable information to users. This is known as the box score and Chapters 4, 5 and 6 will explain the components of a box score.

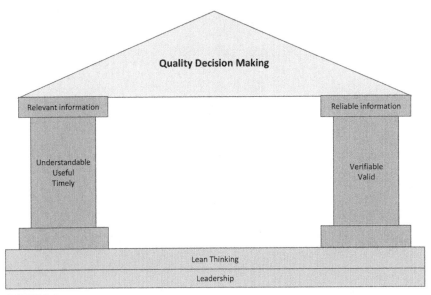

FIGURE 3.9
Architecture of a Lean Management Accounting System

4

Lean Performance Measurements

In this chapter I am going to explain a basic set of lean performance measurements, which can be used in any lean company. The chapter will cover what to measure, how to calculate the measures and how to develop an integrated set of lean performance measurements for a lean company. Later in Chapters 7 and 8 I will explain how these measurements are used in combination with lean practices to control, improve, manage and plan value streams.

One of my earliest "lean lessons" as a CFO was understanding the importance of lean performance measurements in a lean company. Prior to Bullard's lean transformation, we were very traditional when it came to measuring manufacturing operations. We used variances and absorption as our primary operational measurements for both individual jobs and overall operational performance.

Our lean transformation began by hiring a vice president of manufacturing with lean experience, who then hired a team of experienced lean operational managers. One of their first initiatives was to meet with accounting to discuss performance measurements. In a very professional way, they clearly explained to us that they would not be using any variances or absorption numbers as performance measurements. They explained that those measures would not tell them if their improvement goals of reducing lead times and improving quality, delivery and productivity were being achieved. They then asked accounting to partner with them to develop new lean performance measurements because they knew that having accounting's involvement would endorse that the measures were objective, accurate and useful.

DOI: 10.4324/9781003304098-4

Here is what I learned about lean performance measurements from that experience:

- They need to measure real-time process performance.
- The right combination of measures simultaneously measures if a process is delivering value and reveals the waste that is preventing value from being delivered.
- They need to be simple and easy to calculate for the users.
- They need to be reported based on lean management cycles, not accounting reporting periods.
- They are useful to understand the relationships between lean operating performance and financial performance.

Lean performance measurements became an essential tool in Bullard's lean management accounting system. They were used by operations, accounting and senior leadership to learn more about how processes operated, to identify opportunities for improvement and to help everyone better understand how lean operating performance could be leveraged to create financial success.

LEAN PERFORMANCE MEASUREMENT CYCLES

One aspect that distinguishes lean performance measurements from traditional metrics is that they are designed to reveal problems. This means that the frequency of measuring should be based on how fast a process needs to recognize a problem, how fast it must respond to the problem and how long it takes for adjustments to be reflected in process performance. Figure 4.1 summarizes the relationships between the three typical measurement cycles, which we will now look at in detail.

Daily lean performance measurements are designed for cell work teams to measure if the cell is meeting operating performance standards and identify gaps from the standards. Daily measurements are analogous to warning lights on the dashboard of an automobile – if a warning light comes on, the driver must take some action. In the case of daily lean measurements, cell teams must respond when there is a gap from standard by taking corrective action to eliminate the gap.

Category	Daily measures	Weekly measures	Monthly measures
Level	Cell or process	Value stream	Company/division/business unit
Purpose	Meet performance standards	Measure improvement	Assess strategic initiatives
Owners/users	Cell or process teams	Value stream teams	Senior leadership team
"Check & adjust"	Daily huddle	Weekly meeting	Monthly meeting
Number of measures	3 - 5	5 - 7	5 - 7
Improvement	Just-do-its	Kaizen and value stream improvements	Strategy deployment improvement initiatives

FIGURE 4.1
Lean Performance Measurement Cycles

Cell teams respond to gaps from standard in these ways:

- Troubleshooting – as gaps arise, standard responses are enabled to provide short-term countermeasures to deal with the specific issue.
- Just Do It improvements – for recurring problems and issues, teams employ PDCA to enable improvements.

In some processes, the speed with which a team must respond to gaps may require more frequent measurement, which would mean creating an hourly standard. Measuring hourly is called "day by the hour." In other processes, such as software development, a cell team may have more time to respond to gaps, which would mean creating a weekly standard, but checking daily. This is known as "week by the day."

Weekly lean performance measurements are designed for value stream teams to measure overall value stream performance against improvement targets – achieving a new standard of performance. Weekly lean performance measurements answer the question: "Is the value stream making progress towards an improved future state?" If weekly measurements are not trending in the right direction, value stream teams must make the necessary adjustments to their improvement activities.

Monthly lean performance measurements are typically used at the company or division level by management teams to assess the overall lean strategy and associated initiatives. Monthly lean performance measurements indicate to senior leaders if progress is being made towards strategic objectives, which are usually established in the annual strategy deployment process.

If monthly measurements are not trending in the right direction, management teams will make the necessary adjustments to initiatives and tactics.

These relationships are guidelines, and not hard fast rules. For example, in a process where the production cycle time is long, such as software development or building complex machinery, daily measurements to identify gaps from standards may be too frequent, and it may be more logical to measure gaps from standards on a weekly basis. A general rule of thumb is the shorter the total cycle time of the process, the more frequently it should be measured.

Now let's look at specifically what aspects of process performance should be measured.

WHAT TO MEASURE

As mentioned earlier, the right combination of lean performance measurements can give a complete picture of lean process performance. What's great about lean performance measurements is that you can get a pretty complete picture using five to seven measurements in most cases. Figure 4.2 lists the seven categories of process performance that lean companies strive to achieve.

Category	Purpose of measuring
Delivery	Meet customers' delivery expectations
Quality	Meet customers' quality expectations
Lead time/Flow	Flow through a process as fast as possible
Productivity	Increase output of a process with same resources
Cost	Reduce costs over time
Safety	Safe workplace
Morale/Respect for people	People are our most important asset

FIGURE 4.2
Lean Performance Measurement Categories

Performance measurements related to delivery, quality and lead time should be based solely on customer expectations, not the capabilities of a process. Focusing these measures on customer expectations will reveal the right problems to solve to improve delivering value to customers.

Performance measurements related to productivity, cost, and lead time (again) should focus on stretch improvement goals over time, which reveal the waste to eliminate through continuous improvement.

Performance measurements related to safety, morale and respect for people are based on the fact that lean companies recognize that a stable, skilled and educated workforce is the key to a successful lean transformation.

Now let's look at specific daily, weekly and monthly performance measures and how to calculate them.

DAILY OR CELL LEAN PERFORMANCE MEASUREMENTS

Figure 4.3 summarizes the typical daily lean performance measurements which can be applied to any work cell, in any process. Using Figure 4.3 as a guide, let's review some typical daily lean performance measurements in detail.

Category	Typical Measure	Formula
Delivery	Schedule attainment	• Actual work completed / planned work
Quality	Defect rate	• Defective items / total items
Lead time/Flow	Schedule attainment	
	Work in process flow	• Actual cell inventory / planned cell inventory
Productivity	Schedule attainment	
Cost	Drivers of costs	• Overtime hours / total hours • Average changeover time • Operational equipment effectiveness
Safety	Incident rate	• Safety cross
Respect for people	Morale	• Cross training/skill matrix • Problems solved per person • Daily morale check

FIGURE 4.3
Daily Lean Performance Measurements for Cells

Schedule Attainment

Lean companies strive to be make-to-order, which means producing to specific customer demand. Schedule attainment is simply a discrete measure to determine if a cell produced to plan. The planned work can be tangible products completed or on-time delivery of services. In cases where the cycle time of a cell to complete a product or service is longer than a day (such as software development), the planned work can be based on specific progress that needs to be made daily.

Quality

Measuring quality on a daily basis is necessary because lean companies strive to prevent defects from being passed on to customers, which can be the company's customers or downstream processes from cells. This is done by building in "quality-at-the-source" into cell activities, which is the ability for employees to identify defects as fast as possible in order to:

1. Build short-term "stop and fix" countermeasures to prevent defects from being passed on to subsequent cells.
2. Identify the root causes of defects to make improvements to prevent defects from occurring.

Cost

A cell's ability to control costs is based on its understanding of the operating practices that drive costs. Daily lean performance measurements of cost focus on the operational drivers of costs in work cells.

For example, if a cell team is working overtime, but the cell has been properly staffed based on demand, it is important for the cell team to reveal the operational reasons for overtime. Likewise in a machine-based cell, it may be necessary to measure drivers such as downtime, changeover time or operational equipment effectiveness on a daily basis to reveal the drivers of costs.

Flow

Pull systems are designed to have a standard level of work-in-process inventory to maintain flow. A daily measure of flow is designed for a cell team to measure gap from standard work-in-process inventory. This measure may not necessarily mean counting cell work-in-process inventory frequently. It could be a visual system that indicates when cell work-in-process inventory is greater or less than standard. If this occurs, it is a signal to the cell to take the necessary corrective action. This measure is also known as WIP-to-SWIP (actual work-in-process to standard work-in-process).

Here are some examples. In a customer support function, the standard level of support tickets that are in process by any representative could be set at five. If actual tickets are less than five, it is a signal that more tickets need to be pulled by the representative. If actual tickets are more than five, it is a signal that the representative may need help to close the tickets.

Safety

Lean companies consider their employees to be their most important asset and they strive to achieve a safe work environment. The goal of measuring safety is that safety awareness becomes part of everyone's everyday work. Safety measures are usually based on specific incidents and also near misses, which are clearly defined in a company's safety program. A simple daily performance measurement is what is sometimes known as a safety cross, which has 31 days in the shape of a cross. For each day where there are no incidents, that date is colored green, and if there is an incident, the date is colored red.

Respect for People

Lean companies recognize that high morale of employees is based on creating a culture where employees are engaged and satisfied coming to work every day. There are a variety of measures that can be used to measure morale in a cell. Developing employees' skills through cross-training for the various activities in the cell can increase morale. Tracking continuous improvement participation rates or problems solved per person are other potential measures. It's even possible to do a daily morale check with the team by asking how they feel about their workday.

WEEKLY OR VALUE STREAM LEAN PERFORMANCE MEASUREMENTS

Figure 4.4 summarizes the typical weekly lean performance measurements, which are deployed at the value stream (or administrative process) level to measure overall performance improvement towards a time-bound future state goal. Weekly review of value stream measurements will reveal if improvement activities are having a positive impact on driving the measures towards the future state goals. Weekly review of the measures by the value stream team allows it to adjust improvement activities as needed.

Delivery

On-time delivery is a common performance measurement in many companies, but it is typically measured based on a negotiated "promise date" rather than when the customer *wants* delivery of products or services. Lean companies measure on-time delivery against customer expectations, not negotiated promise dates, because they want to reveal the true problems and issues preventing them from meeting customer expectations.

Category	Typical Measure	Formula
Delivery	On-time delivery to customer request date	• Actual orders shipped or completed / planned orders
Quality	Defect rate	• Defective items / total items through value stream • Sum of cells' first time through rates
Lead time/Flow	Average lead time	• Number of days (ship or completion date) – order date
	Material flow	• Days of inventory = annualized material cost / average inventory
Productivity	Increase output with same resources	• Sales / total hours worked • Value added progress / total hours worked
Cost	Cost reduction over time	• Cost(s) as a % of sales • Average actual cost per unit
Safety	Incident rate	• Incidents per person
Respect for people	Morale	• Improvement event participation rate • Training hours per person

FIGURE 4.4
Weekly Lean Performance Measurements for Value Streams

In the case of value streams with long production cycles, such as construction or software development, it may be necessary to modify the on-time delivery measure to "on-time progress." Products and services with long production cycles are typically managed like projects, broken down into specific phases with due dates. On-time progress is simply measuring if specific weekly tasks have been completed according to the plan.

Quality

The quality measure for a value stream is oftentimes called the "first time through" rate. It measures how many units of work go through the value stream defect- and rework-free. The first time through rate can be calculated from the daily defect rates of each cell in the value stream. Figure 4.5 illustrates how a value stream first time through rate can be calculated in this manner.

Lead Time

Lean companies understand eliminating waste in a value stream will make the value stream faster because the capacity being created can be applied to value added activities and orders are processed faster. Capacity also creates more flexibility to adapt to unplanned changes in demand or for reacting to problems and issues as they arise.

Lead time is total processing time, which is the sum of value added activity time plus non-value added activity time. Continuous improvement activities reduce and eliminate non-value added activity time, which

Cell	Defect rate	First time through rate
Step 1	5%	95% X
Step 2	10%	90% X
Step 3	10%	90% X
Step 4	5%	95% X
Value stream total		= 73%

FIGURE 4.5
First Time Through Calculation

reduces lead times. For this reason, it is critical to measure lead times because it measures the effectiveness of improvement activities.

The lead time of any value stream or process is the average length of time from an order receipt date to the fulfillment date. Here are some examples:

- In manufacturing, lead time is calculated based on order receipt date to shipment date.
- In healthcare, lead time is typically measured as length of stay.
- In a service business, such as a repair business, it would be measured from when the customer arrives to when the repairs are completed.
- In an accounting firm it could be calculated based on when a client delivers information for a tax return to when the tax return is completed.

Flow

In companies that maintain an inventory of parts to produce (such as manufacturing) or supplies to use (such as healthcare) it's important to measure material flow using days of inventory. Lean companies that maintain inventory strive to minimize the number of days the inventory is in the business through better purchasing practices, pull systems in production and other lean practices.

Productivity

Productivity is the essence of lean: increase output with the same (or fewer) resources. Output is increased by serving customers better. Resource utilization improves because more time is spent on serving customers and less time is spent on other activities. Productivity and lead time can be considered corollary performance measurements because measuring both helps move each of them in the right direction.

In value streams, the typical productivity measure is sales divided by total hours worked. However, in some value streams that have long cycle times and in which sales are periodic (such as large equipment manufacturing, some professional services and construction) a substitute numerator can be value added progress. This numerator could be based on the specific weekly tasks that have been completed.

Cost

A lean strategy will have a positive impact on managing costs over time, but not through conventional cost-cutting initiatives that non-lean companies employ. Rather, lean focuses on understanding the specific root causes of costs and eliminate them over time.

- Actual cost savings will be realized because improvement activities reduce wastes that have specific costs, such as reducing scrap by improving quality.
- The capacity created through improvement activities can be utilized and this will avoid future cost increases. A simple example is not having to hire additional employees to meet an increase in demand.

Recommended lean performance measurements of cost that will consider both methods of how lean reduces costs are:

- Cost as a percentage of sales – over time, costs increase at a lower rate than sales.
- Contribution margin percentage – which will reflect improvements in variable costs.
- Actual costs per unit – which will be reduced over time because costs increase at a lower rate than the increase in units.

A final note about lean performance measurements of cost. It usually takes time to "move the measure" because it takes time to develop regular continuous improvement activities. Continuous improvement is based on people studying and learning about processes, which takes time, and is also limited because regular work also has to be done. It's important to take a long-term view of cost reduction and not fall into conventional short-term financial thinking of expecting to quickly see improved financial results.

Safety and Respect for People

The specific measures illustrated in Figure 4.4 are similar to the daily lean performance measures in terms of calculation. At the value stream level, what is different is developing improvement targets for these measures and the initiatives that will move the measures towards the targets.

MONTHLY OR COMPANY LEAN PERFORMANCE MEASUREMENTS

Figure 4.6 summarizes the typical monthly lean performance measurements, which are deployed at a company, division, or business unit level to measure its performance towards strategic lean-based goals. These monthly measurements typically become part of monthly leadership meetings and are used to measure the effectiveness and impact of strategic initiatives. If progress is not being made towards the targets, that is an indication senior leaders may have to adjust initiatives and tactics.

The formulae for the measures listed in Figure 4.6 are very similar to the weekly value stream measures in Figure 4.4 that were explained earlier, with a few exceptions which will now be explained.

At a company or division level, it is difficult to have a lean-based quality measure with short feedback loops to understand quality problems in a timely manner. This is why lean companies focus measuring quality where the work gets done, at the cell and value stream level. However, if customers discovering quality problems is an issue for a company, an effective monthly quality performance measurement can be complaints, returns or warranty claims, which can be used by senior leaders to assess overall quality initiatives.

Category	Typical Measure	Formula
Delivery	On-time delivery to customer request date	• Actual orders shipped or completed/ planned orders
Quality	Defect rate	• Customer complaint rate • Warranty or return rate
Lead time/Flow	Average lead time	• Number of days (ship or completion date)– order date
	Material flow	• Days of inventory = annualized material cost / average inventory
Productivity	Increase output with same resources	• Sales / number of employees
Cost	Cost reduction over time	• Cost(s) as a % of sales • Actual gross margin %
Safety	Incident rate	• Incidents per person
Respect for people	Morale	• Improvement event participation rate • Training hours per person • Retention rate

FIGURE 4.6
Monthly Lean Performance Measurements for the Company

The recommended measure of productivity on a monthly basis is sales per employee, based on the total number of employees in the company. This is an effective measurement to assess the overall impact of lean in both operations and administrative functions.

Now let's look at how to create an integrated set of lean performance measurements at all three levels of measurements and how to align them with the company's lean strategy and actions.

THE LINKAGE CHART PROCESS

A Linkage Chart is developed through a standard process following the PDCA cycle. The goal of the process is to develop an integrated set of lean performance measurements that are aligned with a lean strategy, effective in identifying problems, and drive improvement. The steps the process generally follows are:

- Develop the Linkage Chart and do initial calculation of the measurements (Plan).
- Pilot using the measures (Do).
- Review the effectiveness of the measurements (Check).
- Replace ineffective measurements and/or end pilot (Adjust).

Develop the Linkage Chart

A cross-functional team should create the Linkage Chart. The team should consist of the users of the measurements – senior leaders for monthly measurements, value stream managers for weekly measurements and cell leaders for daily measurements. I highly recommend developing a Linkage Chart using a kaizen event approach (one or two days) where the team dedicates the time to complete its development.

Figure 4.7 illustrates a Linkage Chart for a manufacturing company and Figure 4.8 illustrates one for a service company. Using these figures as a guide, the Linkage Chart is developed from left to right. Identify goals and candidate measurements for monthly measurements and link them using arrows. Next, do the same for the weekly measurements with the added

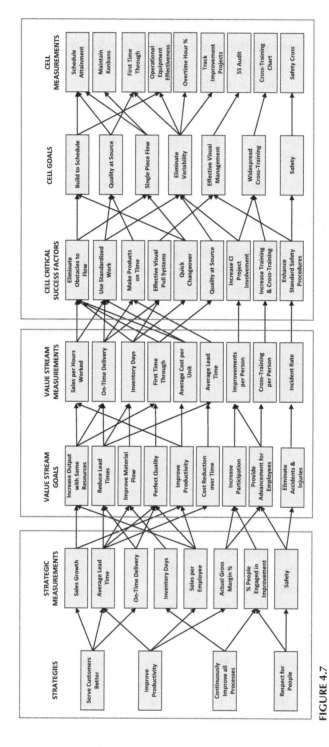

FIGURE 4.7
Linkage Chart for Manufacturing

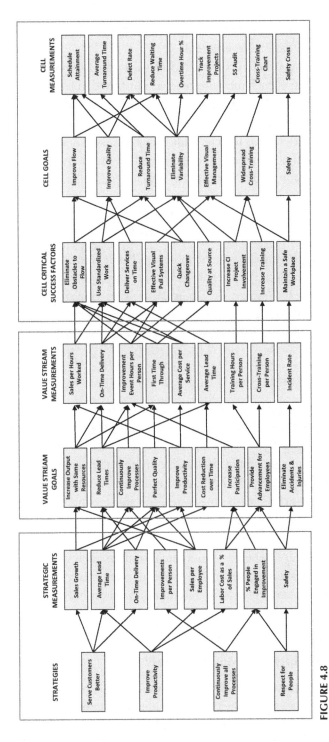

FIGURE 4.8

Linkage Chart for Service

step of linking the monthly measurements to the weekly goals. Finally, do the same for the daily measurements.

After the Linkage Chart is completed, the next step for the team is to do an initial calculation of each measurement, as illustrated in Figure 4.9 (Linkage Chart Event Phase). Each measurement must be specifically defined, then determine how the measure will be calculated and the source of the data. The goal of this exercise is to determine if each measure is simple and easy to gather and calculate. Typically, the team will find that some of the measures may need to be adjusted to make them simpler and easier.

USE POST-IT NOTES!

Make the Linkage Chart visible by using Post-It Notes on paper hung on a wall because as the team develops the chart changes will be made. Also draw the linking arrows in pencil in case they need to be changed. After the Linkage Chart is completed, it can be converted into a more formal-looking document using Excel or another application.

Pilot the Measurements

The next step is to have the owners of the measures pilot the actual use of the measurements, as illustrated in Figure 4.9 (pilot phase). Think of the pilot phase as "practice" by incorporating the measures into daily, weekly and monthly management cycles to determine if they are truly effective in revealing the root causes of both good and poor performance. The more frequent the reporting of the measures, the shorter the pilot phase. Here are some pilot time recommendations:

- Daily measurements for about one month in a few cells.
- Weekly measurements for 4–6 weeks in one or two value streams.
- Monthly measurements for 3–6 months in monthly senior leadership meetings.

Review and Adjust the Measurements

Reviewing the effectiveness of the measurements is ongoing through the pilot phase. Besides their effectiveness in identifying the root causes of performance, the following aspects should also be reviewed:

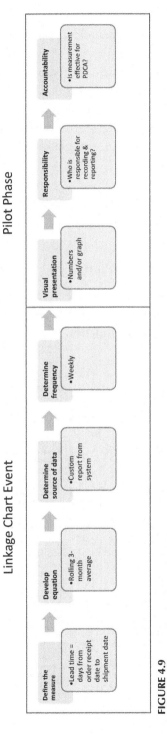

FIGURE 4.9
Steps to Develop Effective Lean Performance Measurements

- Ownership – have teams assumed ownership of the measurements?
- Relevance – are the measures relevant to both the lean strategy and the process being measured?
- Alignment – are the measures aligned with lean operating practices and improvement activities?
- Rationalization – are there other existing measures being used which should not be used any longer? The purpose of a Linkage Chart is to rationalize the performance measurement system, not add more measures!

Performance measurements deemed ineffective may have to be modified or possibly be replaced. Expect to encounter this during the pilot phase.

Linkage Chart Development Plan

Linkage Charts can be developed for every value stream and administrative function in the company. Figures 4.10 and 4.11 illustrate a Linkage Chart for a sales and marketing function. Figure 4.12 illustrates one for a

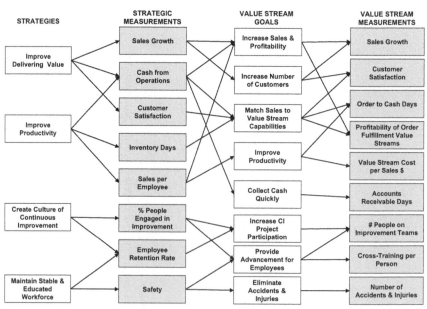

FIGURE 4.10
Linkage Chart for Sales and Marketing

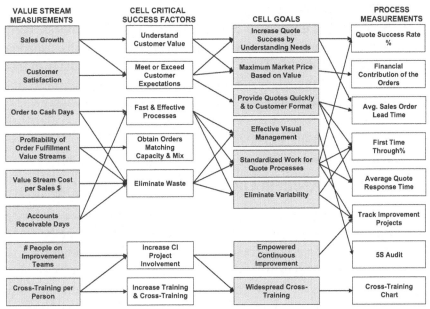

FIGURE 4.11
Linkage Chart for Quote Process in Sales and Marketing

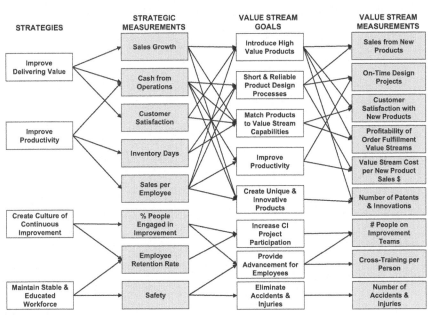

FIGURE 4.12
Linkage Chart for New Product Development

product development process. It's best to develop Linkage Charts as lean practices are being introduced into each process in the business. Early introduction of lean performance measurements in a lean transformation helps employees understand their intended use – to be integrated with lean practices and used to understand process performance, identify problems and measure improvement.

WRAP UP – LEAN PERFORMANCE MEASUREMENTS

Lean performance measurements have been around as long as lean thinking has been around! Read any book about lean and there will probably be some discussion about performance measurements. What's important to understand from a lean management accounting system perspective is that these measurements are an integral component of the system and their use, in combination with lean practices, will control, improve, plan and manage value streams. The application and use of lean performance measurements are covered in Chapters 7 and 8.

Next let's look at the next component of a box score, capacity.

5

Measuring Capacity

TIME IS MONEY

"Time is money" is an expression we've all heard or used many times. It means "don't squander or waste time because it's a valuable resource that needs to be spent wisely." In lean companies, this is how lean leaders view time, as a valuable resource. Their focus is on getting all employees to spend more time serving customers better and less time on everything else. This means that in order to support lean, a lean management accounting system needs to measure time accordingly. This is called measuring capacity.

I consider measuring capacity one of the most vital components of a lean management accounting system. That is because it helps establish the true cause–effect relationships between lean operating performance and financial performance. How a company spends its time goes a long way towards determining how much money it will make. Aligning measuring capacity with lean requires new numbers, based on how lean companies view the use of time. Any work activity either adds value or it does not. While this view may seem stark, and very "black or white," it serves the purpose of getting people to think differently about their work activities and seek opportunities to improve.

I have found the best way to learn how to measure capacity for a lean management accounting system is to see how it is calculated. But before we get to the actual number crunching, let's review the economics of lean and take a deeper dive into how lean companies categorize work activities.

DOI: 10.4324/9781003304098-5

THE ECONOMICS OF LEAN

Figure 5.1 illustrates the economics of lean and the relationships between capacity and financial performance. The primary outcome of continuous improvement is eliminating waste, which means it creates capacity. In other words, employees have more capacity to do more or other work because they are not performing wasteful activities.

LABOR IS AN ASSET!

In financial accounting, an asset is defined as a resource with economic value that a company owns or controls with the expectation that it will provide a future benefit. Assets such as equipment or buildings meet this definition and are capitalized on the balance sheet. Yet the cost of employees is recorded as an expense on the income statement even though employees also meet the definition of an asset. Even though financial accounting standards cannot be changed, you can change thinking inside your company with a lean management accounting system.

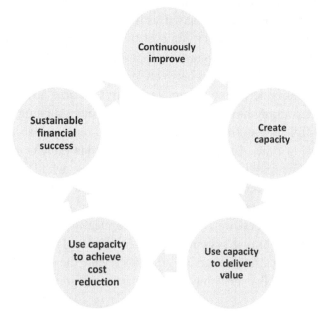

FIGURE 5.1
Economics of Lean

The financial impact of continuous improvement is based upon how this freed-up capacity is used. If available capacity is used to create value for customers, such as shorter lead times and higher on-time delivery, this can have a positive impact on sales. In many lean companies, the application of available capacity to create value also creates a competitive advantage.

Available capacity can also be used to achieve long-term cost reduction. For example, enough capacity may be created over time to reduce overtime, which reduces costs. Available capacity can also be used to avoid costs, such as not having to buy additional equipment or hire additional people.

Here is how I learned firsthand about the economics of lean and that "time is money," as CFO of Bullard.

Before embarking on a lean transformation, Bullard was profitable and had steady growth, but order fulfillment lead times were inconsistently long, and on-time delivery was not up to customer expectations. When we embarked on our lean transformation, we set three goals:

- ship every order in three days or less;
- on-time delivery 95% or better;
- eliminate finished goods inventory.

These were daunting goals, which seemed impossible to reach based on where we were and how our processes performed. It took us about three years, but after having improvement events focused on establishing make-to-order pull systems, improving quality and reducing changeover times, we achieved all three goals. Our financial performance was something we never dreamed of:

- Sales, which previously grew 5–7% annually, now were growing over 20% because we had the shortest lead times and highest on-time delivery in the industry.
- The annual growth rate of costs, which was typically 4–6%, remained the same.
- Cash flow increased and Bullard paid off all debt.

TYPES OF ACTIVITIES

Earlier I wrote that lean companies divide all activities into those that add value and those that do not. Measuring capacity in lean management accounting is based on being able to identify activities as either value added or non-value added. Every activity in a process, whether it be a complete process step or tasks within process steps, can be categorized into one of three types of activities – value added; and two types of non-value added activities: non-value added but necessary or non-value added and wasteful activities. Here is how to identify each type of activity.

Value Added Activities

Value added activities are those which must be performed to deliver a tangible product or an intangible product (such as information) or to complete a service. Value added activities *must* be performed to meet customer requirements. In manufacturing this is usually called the cycle time to produce a product. In service businesses, it is the direct interaction between an employee and a customer. In administrative functions, it is the required activities to transform information to generate the output. Not performing a value added activity directly impacts the quality of the product or service delivered to the customer.

Non-Value Added but Necessary Activities

These activities don't create value for the customer but must be performed for a specific business reason. Another way to think of non-value added but necessary activities is that they are required activities which must be performed to support the company or processes. Here are some examples. In healthcare, there are many activities which must occur for regulatory reasons, such as providers ordering services in a specific manner to treat patients. In manufacturing, raw materials must be purchased to be used by value streams. In all companies, there is a process to follow when hiring employees.

Non-value added but necessary activities cannot be eliminated, but how they are performed can be improved upon because waste may exist *in how* they are performed. Lean companies strive to "lean out" non-value added but necessary activities.

Productive capacity	• total time spent on value added activities
Non-productive capacity	• total time spent on all non-value added activities: necessary activities and wasteful activities
Available capacity	• total time created through continuous improvement

FIGURE 5.2
Capacity and Activities

Non-Value Added and Wasteful Activities

These activities are known in lean as the eight types of waste – defects, overproduction, waiting time, neglect of talent, transportation, inventory, motion, and excess processing. These activities can be eliminated with no impact on serving customers or meeting business requirements.

Figure 5.2 summarizes the relationship between measures of capacity and activities. Measuring capacity in this manner aligns with the economics of lean and gives users the ability to measure both the short-term and long-term impacts of lean in box scores. In the short term, the impact of improvement activities that create capacity can be measured. In the long term, the financial impact of how the available capacity is utilized can be measured in a box score.

Understanding the differences between value added and non-value added activities is necessary when collecting the data to do the calculation of capacity.

PROCESS ANALYSIS AND DATA COLLECTION

In order to calculate capacity, data on the value added and non-value added activities must be collected. If value stream maps or process maps have been prepared in a standard manner with data boxes, as illustrated in Figure 5.3, they usually contain much of the necessary information to calculate capacity.

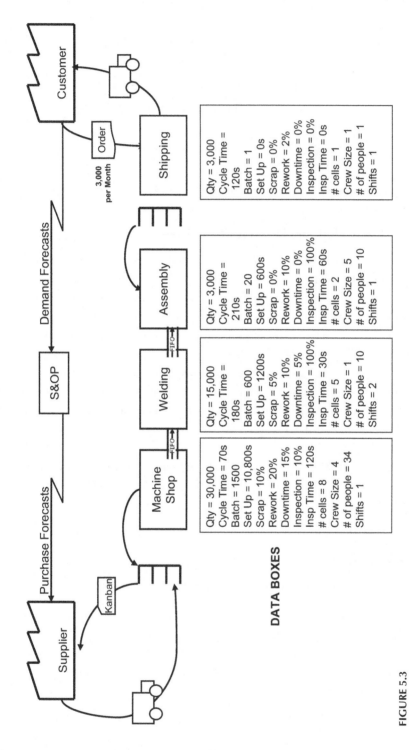

DATA BOXES

FIGURE 5.3
Value Stream Map with Data Boxes

If value stream or process maps are not available, it's necessary to collect data through direct observation, a "lean time study." Two questions arise when data must be collected:

- How long do we need to observe?
- How much data do we collect on the process steps?

Ideally it would be good to collect 30 observations. But one must consider the time and effort to get 30 observations. If processing times in a value stream are short, for example total processing time can be calculated in minutes, it's relatively easy to get 30 observations. When processing times are longer, such as hours or days, it may be more practical to do fewer observations.

OBSERVE, DON'T ASK

I highly recommend that the data collection process be completed through direct observation, rather than asking employees who work in the process what they think. Employees who work in the process may not understand lean and lean views of activities. This means they may confuse value added and non-value added activities when giving responses. They may also respond by giving "best case" answers. Asking people what they think will lead to biased responses.

The goal is to collect data on every process step, but that may be impractical for value streams with many process steps, where the time and effort to collect the data may outweigh the benefit. An alternative method to collecting data on every process step is to collect data on the bottleneck process step(s). The definition of a bottleneck is the process step with the longest value-added cycle time. Bottlenecks control the rate of flow for the entire value stream. For example, if the cycle time of the bottleneck step of a value stream is 10 minutes, this means the value stream output is limited to 6 units per hour (60 minutes divided by 10 minutes).

Because bottlenecks control the rate of flow for a whole value stream, it is possible to calculate the capacity for the bottleneck process because its capacity controls the capacity of the entire value stream. Measuring capacity of bottlenecks can greatly reduce the data collection effort.

Now it's time to do some number crunching and illustrate exactly how capacity is measured by process activity and by position activity.

DATA COLLECTION METHODS

The two methods to collect the required data to measure capacity are based on the process activities or the position activities and are summarized in Figure 5.4. While Figure 5.4 makes a distinction between products and services, please remember these are guidelines not hard fast rules.

Data Collection on Process Activities

This is the recommended method to use for processes that produce tangible products where the process steps are standardized and must be performed in a specific sequence. Failure to perform the process steps in the required sequence means the product will not meet quality standards. Examples of when to use this method of data collection to calculate capacity are manufacturing value streams and testing laboratories.

Data Collection on Position Activities

This is the recommended method to use for processes that deliver services. When delivering services, there is a process which must be completed, but the exact sequence of these activities may vary a bit based on the interaction with the customer. For example, nurses have a group of patients to

Data collection	Output	Process
Process step activities	Tangible product	Must be completed in a specific sequence
Employee position activities	Service performed	Sequence completed based on interaction with customer

FIGURE 5.4
Data Collection Methods for Capacity

serve at the same time and may have to adjust their work routines based on current patient needs.

It's also recommended to use this method of data collection for administrative processes based on the varied responsibilities of employees who work in these processes. For example, in human resources, a team member may work in the hiring process, the benefits management process and also deal with employee questions during a typical day, all based on specific interactions as they occur.

Let's now look at an example of each data collection method.

Example: Measuring Capacity by Process Activities

The Provalve value stream produces a product family that consists of five different products. The value stream consists of three steps – fabricating the four components, machining the four components and assembling the components into the final product. Fabricating work is done on eight machines and each machine has an operator. Machining is done on five machines, and each machine has an operator. The six employees in final assembly assemble the four component parts into the final products.

The value stream has a current state value stream map with data boxes and that data is going to be used to calculate capacity following these five steps:

1. Calculate total available time.
2. Calculate value added time and productive capacity.
3. Calculate non-value added time, waste time.
4. Calculate non-value but necessary time and non-productive capacity.
5. Calculate available capacity.

Now let's look at each step in detail, where I will explain some options and choices that may have to be considered.

Step 1: Calculate Total Available Time (Figure 5.5)

The first step in measuring capacity is to calculate total available time, which will serve as the denominator in calculating the capacity percentages. This step includes an important decision point which is to determine the resource that performs the value added work in each process step. In the case of the fabricating and machining operations, machines perform

	Fabrication	Machining	Assembly	Value Stream Total
Total available time				
Resource performing work	Machines	Machines	People	
Number of resources	8	5	6	
Shift hours	8	8	8	
Number of shifts	1	1	1	
Lunch and break time (minutes)	60	60	60	
Days in the month	20	20	20	
Total available time	67,200	42,000	50,400	159,600

FIGURE 5.5
Calculating Total Available Time

the value added work, while in assembly employees perform the value added work.

The shift hours entered should be based on a standard shift. You have the option of including average overtime hours here if you want. For the remaining information, use what is considered "current."

Figure 5.5 summarizes the calculation of 159,600 minutes total available time, based on the number of resources and one eight-hour shift over 20 working days a month.

Step 2: Calculate Value Added Time and Productive Capacity (Figure 5.6)

The total value added time is calculated by multiplying the cycle time per unit in each operation by the number of units produced. Value streams typically produce a family of products, which can have variations in cycle times and units. If this is the case, you may have to consider using some sort of average for both inputs.

A simple average of cycle time and units can be used in value streams that have a small family of products. In value streams with a larger family of products, you may have to consider using a weighted average or use the 80/20 rule, and average only the cycle times and units for the products that contribute the majority of production volume.

Figure 5.6 summarizes the calculation of the productive capacity of 40% for the value stream as well as each of the three process steps.

Value added time	Fabrication	Machining	Assembly	Value Stream Total
Units shipped	8,000	8,000	2,000	
Cycle time per unit	3	3	8	
Total value added time	24,000	24,000	16,000	64,000
Productive capacity %	36%	57%	32%	40%

FIGURE 5.6
Calculating Productive Capacity

Non-productive, waste time	Fabrication	Machining	Assembly	Value Stream Total
Batch size	30	10		
Total parts made	10,000	10,000	3,333	
Number of changeovers	333	1,000		
Time per changeover	20	3		
Total changeover time	6,667	3,000		9,667
Scrap rate	20%	20%	40%	
Scrap quantity	2,000	2,000	1,333	
Total scrap time	6,000	6,000	10,667	22,667
Percentage of items inspected	25%	25%	50%	
Total parts made	10,000	10,000	3,333	
Inspection time per unit	1	0.5	6	
Total inspection time	2,500	1,250	10,000	13,750
Downtime percentage	10%	10%	10%	
Total available time	67,200	42,000	50,400	
Total downtime	6,720	4,200	5,040	15,960

FIGURE 5.7
Calculating Non-Productive, Waste Time

Step 3: Calculate Non-Value Added, Waste Time (Figure 5.7)

A value stream mapping process quantifies certain types of waste such as defects, changeover times, downtime, overproduction and inspection times. This information can be used to calculate the non-value added, wasteful time for measuring capacity.

This information can be used to calculate capacity as follows:

- Changeover time is the number of changeovers multiplied by the time per changeover.
- Overproduction time is the quantity overproduced multiplied by the cycle time.
- Scrap and rework time is the scrap and rework quantity multiplied by the cycle time.
- Inspection time is the number of units inspected multiplied by inspection time per unit.
- Downtime is the total available time multiplied by the downtime percentage.

Figure 5.7 summarizes the non-value added, waste time for the Provalve value stream, based on:

- Changeover time in fabrication and machining.
- Scrap in all three process steps.

- Quality inspection in all three process steps.
- Downtime in all three process steps.

Step 4: Calculate Non-Productive but Necessary Time and Non-Productive Capacity (Figure 5.8)

These types of activities must be specifically identified based on what are considered "necessary" business activities for any value stream. In the Provalve value stream there are two non-value added but necessary activities that occur each day: 15 minutes of 5-S activities and a 15-minute daily huddle. While these activities occur, the machines in fabrication and assembly are not operating. It's also possible to include improvement activities as part of non-value added but necessary activities. In the case of the Provalve value stream, each employee spends eight hours per month on various improvement events.

Figure 5.8 summarizes the calculation of non-productive capacity for the Provalve value stream, which is the total of the non-value waste and necessary activity time. The value stream also separated continuous improvement capacity in their presentation.

When presenting non-productive capacity, you have options. In the example of the Provalve value stream, they added both types of

	Fabrication	Machining	Assembly	Value Stream Total
Non-productive, waste time				
Total changeover time	6,667	3,000		9,667
Total scrap time	6,000	6,000	10,667	22,667
Total inspection time	2,500	1,250	10,000	13,750
Total downtime	6,720	4,200	5,040	15,960
Non-productive but necessary activities				
Number of people	8	5	6	
Daily time in 5-S and huddles per person	30	30	30	
Total non-productive but necessary time	4,800	3,000	3,600	11,400
Total non-productive time	26,687	17,450	29,307	73,444
Non-productive capacity %	40%	42%	58%	46%
Continuous improvement activities				
Number of people	8	5	6	
Time per month per person (hours)	8	8	8	
Continuous improvement time	3,840	2,400	2,880	9,120
Continuous improvement capacity %	6%	6%	6%	6%
AVAILABLE CAPACITY %	19%	-4%	4%	8%

FIGURE 5.8
Calculating Non-Productive Capacity

	Fabrication	Machining	Assembly	Value Stream Total
Total available time	67,200	42,000	50,400	159,600
Total value added time	24,000	24,000	16,000	64,000
Productive capacity %	**36%**	**57%**	**32%**	**40%**
Total non-productive time	26,687	17,450	29,307	73,444
Non-productive capacity %	**40%**	**42%**	**58%**	**46%**
Continuous improvement activities				
Number of people	8	5	6	
Time per month per person (hours)	8	8	8	
Continuous improvement time	3,840	2,400	2,880	9,120
Continuous improvement capacity %	**6%**	**6%**	**6%**	**6%**
AVAILABLE CAPACITY %	**19%**	**-4%**	**4%**	**8%**

FIGURE 5.9
Calculating Available Capacity

non-productive activity time together to arrive at 46% non-productive capacity. Another option would be to show the capacity percentages for the two types of non-productive activities separately.

The available capacity of the value stream, and each process step, is calculated simply by subtracting the productive, non-productive and continuous improvement capacity percentages from 100%, as illustrated in Figure 5.9.

The Provalve capacity calculation provides insight into where to possibly focus future improvement efforts. Improving quality in all process steps will reduce both scrap and inspection activities. Implementing total productive maintenance will reduce downtime in all process steps.

Example: Measuring Capacity by Position Activities

In service value streams, there are standard activities which must be completed, but the exact sequence of these activities may vary a bit based on the interaction with the customer. For capacity calculation purposes, it's best to do direct process observation for data collection since it may be difficult to draw a value stream map.

Figure 5.10 summarizes the activities for a team of nurses in an inpatient wing of a small regional hospital. The value added activities are those that contribute directly to the patients' plans of care. The necessary activities are those which must be performed, but do not directly contribute to the patients' plans of care. The non-productive activities are viewed as waste and can be eliminated without impacting value added or necessary activities.

Activity	Quantity	Cycle time	Type of activity
Rounds/check-ins	450	20	Value added
Treatment	300	30	Value added
Update records	150	15	Value added
Searching for supplies	360	15	Non-productive
Messages	200	10	Non-productive
Phone calls	300	10	Non-productive
Meetings	60	30	Non-productive
Intake	150	30	Necessary
Rooming	150	30	Necessary
Discharge	125	60	Necessary
Coding	150	15	Necessary

FIGURE 5.10
Summary of Nurses' Activities

Position information	Quantity
Number of nurses	4
Hours per day	8
Days per month	30
Total available time	57,600

FIGURE 5.11
Calculating Total Available Time

Using the data from Figure 5.10, capacity for the team of nurses can be calculated following the same five steps explained in the previous section.

Step 1: Calculate Total Available Time (Figure 5.11)

This team decided it would calculate capacity based on the first shift of a workday. A team of four nurses work this eight-hour shift, and Figure 5.11 summarizes the calculation of total available time of 57,600 minutes per month. This will serve as the denominator to calculate the capacity percentages.

Step 2: Calculate Value Added Time and Productive Capacity (Figure 5.12)

During the process observation and data collection activities, three value added activities were identified:

1. Rounds – 450 rounds per month and each round takes 20 minutes to complete.

2. Treatments – 300 treatments per month and each treatment takes 30 minutes to complete.
3. Updating records – patient records were updated 150 times and each update took 15 minutes to complete.

Figure 5.12 summarizes the calculation of total value added time of 20,250 minutes and the productive capacity of 35%.

Step 3: Calculate Non-Value Added but Necessary Time and Capacity (Figure 5.13)

During the process observation and data collection activities, four non-productive but necessary activities were identified:

1. Intake – 150 patient intakes are completed, and each intake takes 30 minutes to complete.
2. Rooming – the same 150 patients are roomed, and each rooming takes 30 minutes to complete.

Value added time	Quantity	Cycle time	Total time
Rounds/check-ins	450	20	9,000
Treatment	300	30	9,000
Update records	150	15	2,250
Total value added time			20,250
Total available time			57,600
Productive capacity			35%

FIGURE 5.12
Calculating Productive Capacity

Necessary time	Quantity	Cycle time	Total time
Intake	150	30	4,500
Rooming	150	30	4,500
Discharge	125	60	7,500
Coding	150	15	2,250
Total necessary time			18,750
Total available time			57,600
Necessary capacity			33%

FIGURE 5.13
Calculating Necessary Capacity

3. Discharge – 125 patients are discharged, and each discharge takes 60 minutes to complete.
4. Coding – 150 coding activities are completed, and each takes 15 minutes to complete.

Figure 5.13 summarizes the calculation of necessary time of 18,750 minutes and the necessary capacity of 33%.

Step 4: Calculate Non-Productive Time and Capacity (Figure 5.14)

During the process observation and data collection activities, four non-productive and wasteful activities were identified:

1. Searching for supplies – searching for supplies occurs 360 times per month and takes 15 minutes for each search.
2. Messages – the team must respond to 200 messages per month, each of which takes 10 minutes.
3. Phone calls – the team had 300 phone calls per month, each of which took 10 minutes.
4. Meetings – the team participates in 60 meetings per month, which average about 30 minutes in length.

Figure 5.14 summarizes the calculation of total non-productive and unnecessary time of 12,200 minutes and the non-productive and unnecessary capacity of 21%.

Non-productive time	Quantity	Cycle time	Total time
Searching for supplies	360	15	5,400
Messages	200	10	2,000
Phone calls	300	10	3,000
Meetings	60	30	1,800
Total non-productive time			12,200
Total available time			57,600
Non-productive capacity			21%

FIGURE 5.14
Calculating Non-Productive Capacity

Capacity Summary	Minutes	%
Total available	57,600	100%
Productive capacity	20,250	35%
Necessary capacity	18,750	33%
Non-productive capacity	12,200	21%
Available capacity	6,400	11%

FIGURE 5.15
Calculating Available Capacity

Step 5: Calculate Available Capacity (Figure 5.15)

As summarized in Figure 5.15, the available capacity for this team of nurses is 11%. Calculating capacity reveals that nurses spend over 50% of their time on necessary and non-productive activities. Knowing this information, eliminating the non-productive activities and reducing the waste in the necessary activities will create more capacity for nurses to spend time in direct patient care, which in healthcare is serving customers better.

FREQUENCY OF MEASURING CAPACITY

The best way to think about measuring capacity is that it is the "average capacity" based on the current operating practices. As such, it should be recalculated periodically based on the continuous improvement activity cycle in a value stream.

If a company has a regular cycle of value stream mapping, capacity will be initially measured based on the current state map. It can be re-measured during the next scheduled mapping event using updated information from the "new" current state map. Another option, if improvement activities are regularly scheduled, would be to recalculate capacity quarterly or monthly.

The purpose of re-calculating capacity is to keep the measurement up to date for decision makers to make quality business decisions.

WRAP UP: TIME IS MONEY

It's been my experience, working with lean companies, that those who measure capacity in their lean management accounting systems improve the quality of their decision making. As stated in the introduction to this chapter, time is money, and the more wisely a company spends its time will have a direct impact on how it spends its money and how much money it makes.

As a Lean CFO, it is important to understand that measuring capacity establishes the true cause–effect relationships between lean operating practices and financial performance in a lean management accounting system. Developing a deep understanding of these relationships throughout the company will drive financial improvement over time.

Now let's learn about value stream income statements, the final component of a box score.

6

Value Stream Income Statements

GAAP = GAAH!

This is a typical reaction of non-financial managers in companies when they are given financial reports based on Generally Accepted Accounting Principles (GAAP), and they are expected to explain the financial results. This reaction occurs for three primary reasons:

1. Accounting principles exist to create common standards for external financial reporting, making it easier for readers of financial statements to understand company performance and make rational decisions about investments, loans or comparing companies' financial performance.
2. The reporting requirements of GAAP can mask actual financial performance because of specific adjustments accounting must make to maintain compliance with GAAP.
3. The principles are very technical and are just plain difficult to understand. Even experienced CFOs must occasionally consult with their CPA firms to help them understand how to maintain compliance with GAAP.

The result? Many non-financial managers have a hard time explaining actual operating performance using GAAP-based financial reports. In lean companies, this problem is further exacerbated because GAAP-based financial reports are not modeled on the economics of lean and sometimes "show" that "lean is not working." From a lean point of view, the difficulties

DOI: 10.4324/9781003304098-6

managers have in using GAAP-based financial reports are a problem of poor quality information, that must be solved. Value stream income statements solve these problems.

PURPOSE OF VALUE STREAM INCOME STATEMENTS

A value stream income statement is an internal financial report designed specifically for understanding the true cause–effect relationships between lean operating performance and financial performance. Value stream income statements, when used in conjunction with lean performance measurements and capacity measurements, drive root cause analysis of the operational issues impacting financial performance.

Value stream income statements are designed to meet the needs of different internal users. Value stream teams or managers can use them to better understand the direct impact of value stream performance on the sales and costs they control. Accounting and operations can use value stream income statements to better understand the level of improvement needed to achieve financial goals. Decision makers can use value stream income statements to accurately project the true financial impact of just about every business decision.

In Chapters 7 and 8 I will explain in detail how value stream income statements are used. This chapter will explain how to design value stream income statements for your company.

VALUE STREAMS ARE PROFIT CENTERS

Chapter 3 explained how lean companies organize, manage, improve and control by value streams to serve customers better. Value streams flow horizontally through the traditional organizational structure, making them more important than departments, divisions or business units. From a financial viewpoint, it's important to look at value streams as the profit centers of the company. They generate the revenue by serving customers; they spend money and generate an operating profit. The expenses in any value stream are directly related to its lean operating performance and capacity requirements.

VALUE STREAM INCOME STATEMENT PRACTICES

Value stream income statements must be designed with their users in mind. There is not a specific set of standards which must be met to create a value stream income statement but rather a set of practices to follow. By following these practices, a company can design and format value stream income statements to meet the specific needs of all its users.

Practice 1: Simple Format

Value stream income statements should be easy to read for non-financial users, using everyday language they understand, and also be based on a rational, simple chart of accounts. For example, most users of value stream income statements don't need to see five or six different labor expense line items, where one would suffice. In other lean accounting books this simple format is referred to as "Plain-English financial statements." To simplify the format, consider it a continuous improvement event, which focuses on delivering what the customer wants. This is a simple improvement event – ask the users what level of detail they would like to see.

Practice 2: Report Actual

Value stream income statements should always report actual sales and actual costs incurred for the reporting period. This is important to establish the actual cause–effect relationships between lean operating performance and financial performance. Non-financial managers think about financial performance with more like a "checkbook approach" than a "GAAP mentality." They intuitively understand that sales are simply based on products shipped or services delivered, not revenue recognition practices. They also understand that actual costs are based on spending decisions and operating practices, not complex financial reporting adjustments.

It's important to note here that the definition of "actual" should be based on your method of accounting – accrual or cash. Simply report actual costs based on how expenses are recorded in your general ledger through accounts payable, prepaid expense amortization or any other normal, regular accrual accounting methodology. Avoid using GAAP-based adjustments non-financial managers would not understand, such as accruals for obsolete inventory.

Practice 3: Properly Define Variable and Fixed Costs

The definition of fixed and variable costs is heavily influenced by financial reporting and analytical practices, which can make fixed costs look like variable costs. One example is direct labor in manufacturing where product costing is used. In product costing, the direct labor cost of any product is based on how long it takes to make the product, which gives the illusion that direct labor is a variable cost. Another example is any cost allocation methodology, such as calculating cost per patient in healthcare or cost per customer served in a service business, where the allocation basis creates the impression that costs are variable.

In lean management accounting it is important to adopt simple and standard definitions of variable and fixed costs when designing a value stream income statement. This is important because the proper classification of variable and fixed costs, based on how each cost actually behaves, will improve analytical practices and decision making. Here are the recommended definitions to use:

- Variable costs – costs that vary in direct proportion to changes in short-term sales volume.
- Fixed costs – costs that do not change in direct proportion to changes in short-term sales volume and are influenced by management decisions.

Practice 4: Avoid Cost Allocations

In many companies, cost allocations are commonly used to assign costs to products, jobs, projects, customers and business units for analytical and reporting purposes. Any cost allocation method involves a level of subjectivity in assigning costs, which can be confusing to users. Examples of cost allocation methods are product costing, assigning corporate overhead to divisions, and creating artificial "charges" between departments or divisions. In designing value stream income statements, it is best to avoid including cost allocations because the focus is on the relationship between actual costs and operating performance.

DESIGNING A VALUE STREAM INCOME STATEMENT

Now let's look at how to design a value stream income statement following these practices. Figure 6.1 illustrates a typical format of a value stream income statement and the following paragraphs will explain line-by-line

Value Stream Income Statement		
	Year to date	
Sales	2,001,400	
Direct variable costs		
Raw materials	829,936	
Supplies	6,790	
Outside processing & services	60,043	
Sales commissions	40,028	
Contribution margin	1,064,603	53%
Direct fixed costs		
Labor:		
Salaries and wages	176,890	
Benefits	26,534	
Machines & equipment:		
Depreciation	19,300	
Repairs & maintenance	9,750	
Tooling	2,335	
Other direct fixed costs	12,000	
Total direct fixed costs	246,809	12%
Value stream operating margin	817,795	41%
Shared operating costs		
Support labor	13,670	
Shared production costs	27,540	
Facilities	40,250	
Total shared operating costs	81,460	4%
Value stream operating profit	736,335	37%

FIGURE 6.1
Value Stream Income Statement

the logic behind this format, and the options companies have in designing their formats.

Sales

Being able to identify the sales or revenue for each value stream is fairly straightforward because the process of identifying value streams is usually based on products or services that have similar flow through the company.

Variable Costs

The actual variable costs for any value stream are identified based on those costs which vary in direct proportion to changes in sales. In manufacturing, raw material is a primary variable cost because it varies in direct proportion with every unit sold. In healthcare, the equivalent of raw materials is drugs and supplies, which vary based on the number of patients seen. In restaurants, it is food. In some service value streams, it can be parts and supplies. Some companies even have included sales commissions as value stream variable costs. It's possible in knowledge-based companies, such as software development or professional services, that there may not be significant variable costs.

In companies that have inventory on their balance sheet and cost of goods sold on their income statement, it will be necessary to define "actual material cost." Cost of goods sold is based on financial accounting reporting requirements to comply with the matching principle in financial reporting, which simply means to show the costs associated with the revenue recognized in a reporting period. This is typically accomplished through the use of a product costing system, where the cost of each product sold makes up cost of goods sold.

The lean management accounting perspective of material cost is different. The objective is to show the actual cost of materials consumed or used by a value stream. A recommended approach for reporting actual material cost is to report how much material entered into the value stream in a reporting period (cost of goods sold is how much exited) by showing material purchases or material issued into the value stream from inventory.

Material purchases can be used if two conditions exist. Raw material inventory levels are low, and the different types of raw material are unique to each value stream. In the case where raw material levels are high and/or similar raw materials are used by multiple value streams, it is usually simpler to record raw material issued as actual.

Contribution Margin

Contribution margin is a common calculation in financial analysis and may not be well understood by non-financial managers. It is the revenue available after variable costs to cover fixed costs and provide a profit. In lean management accounting it is a very useful tool in decision making, which will be discussed in detail in Chapter 8.

Fixed Costs

Value stream fixed costs are the actual costs that a value stream has direct control over through its operating practices and the resources assigned to it. The primary fixed costs of most value streams are labor and machine/equipment costs. In any value stream people and/or machines are the resources that perform the value added work to produce a product or deliver a service.

In lean management accounting, a way to look at labor and machine costs is that these costs are how much a value stream is paying for a given level of capacity. This link between actual labor and machine cost and value stream capacity becomes very useful in business decision making and cost management. This will be discussed in detail in Chapter 8.

The best method to determine actual labor and machine costs is using the value stream organization. Labor cost for any value stream is based on the actual employees assigned to that value stream, which includes managers, supervisors and any functional support. Labor cost includes salaries, wages and benefits.

The value stream organization also specifically identifies the machines and equipment in each value stream. The actual machine cost for any value stream can include depreciation, repair and maintenance, tooling and any other cost which can be directly charged to specific machines.

There may be other direct fixed costs for value streams. To determine which other fixed costs may be direct costs, here is the method I use when working with companies in developing value stream income statements. I have a team of people from accounting and operations review all expense line items on the company income statement and understand what is being posted to each expense. The team can then determine if an entire expense line item can be charged to one value stream or whether individual charges in an expense line item should be charged to different value streams. Another beneficial outcome of this exercise is how much everyone learns about what makes up each expense.

Value Stream Operating Margin

Value stream managers or teams have responsibility and accountability for value stream operating margin. They have direct control over generating revenue by flowing orders through the value stream to customers. They control their actual costs through their operating practices, capacity usage and improvement activities. Using box scores, value stream teams quickly learn the relationships between lean performance measures, capacity usage and value stream margin.

Shared Costs

During the process of identifying value streams, lean companies also identify shared resources, which can be thought of as "internal suppliers" of products or services to multiple value streams. Shared resources fall into three categories. A shared resource can perform an operational process, such as a testing lab in a hospital or a production step in manufacturing (oftentimes these are called monuments). A shared resource can also provide a service, such as maintenance, engineering or quality. The final category of shared resources is a company's physical plant, which houses the value streams and administrative functions. While a value stream does not have direct control over its portion of shared costs, it can have an influence on shared costs through its operating practices.

For decision-making purposes, companies can elect to assign a portion of shared costs on each value stream income statement. The first step in assigning shared costs is to gather the actual costs of the shared resources. The second step is to assign shared costs to value streams by a simple, repeatable method to get a reasonable representation of its use of shared resources. Here are some examples of simple, repeatable methods to assign shared costs.

Shared operational process costs can be assigned to value streams based on a usage ratio of each value stream's usage to the total output of the shared process. Because shared process steps are usually value added, the incentive is not for value streams to use less of the shared process step, but for operations to determine if it would be more cost-effective and serve customers better if these "monuments" were broken down and replicated in each value stream.

Support functions that provide services to all value streams are usually the most difficult to assign to value streams because of having to determine a simple method to apportion the costs. It's important to avoid creating a complex system to track how much each value stream "uses" the support functions, such as time tracking.

The recommended approach would be for a small cross-functional team to use a PDCA problem-solving approach to develop a simple assignment method. The team can look at how each support function interacts with value streams in an attempt to come up with a simple assignment method. If a simple assignment method cannot be developed, it may be best not to assign the shared costs.

It is common to assign facility costs to value streams based on the amount of physical space used by each value stream. A value stream can influence total facility costs by reducing its footprint and creating available space for new business. In fact, one company I worked with a few years ago assigned its unused facility space to sales and marketing to incentivize them to grow the business.

Over the years in working with companies, I have seen different approaches to assigning shared costs to value streams. Some companies have used the methods described above. Others decided not to assign shared costs to value streams but to show them separately as "support costs" on a company value stream income statement. Yet others have created their own simple methods to assign shared costs. In determining how best to assign shared costs in your company, keep the method simple and base it on the reasons why you want shared costs assigned to value streams.

Value Stream Operating Profit

The primary reason for including shared costs on value stream income statements is to get a more complete picture of value stream operating profit for decision making. Improving value stream operating profit is more cross-functional than improving value stream margin and usually is done by senior leaders or teams that represent value streams, support functions and finance.

Now let's look at the next step in developing value stream income statements, which is re-formatting a company's income statement into a value stream format.

DESIGNING A COMPANY VALUE STREAM INCOME STATEMENT

Once value stream income statements have been created for all value streams, the next logical step is to re-format the company income statement into a value stream format for internal analytical purposes. (Note: this does not necessarily mean you are changing the format for external reporting purposes.)

Building a company value stream income statement is not difficult once individual value stream income statements have been developed. The design process really boils down to deciding how to show the "rest of the company expenses" and how to reconcile the company value stream income statement to the externally reported profit. A sample company-wide value stream income statement is illustrated in Figure 6.2 and the following paragraphs will explain its development.

The company represented in Figure 6.2 has two value streams – OEM and Systems. In developing each of their value stream income statements, it was decided to call the actual labor for each value stream "direct labor," which includes all employees in each value stream. The line item "support labor" refers to the shared costs of operational support functions used by both value streams. Another shared cost is facilities, which is assigned to each value stream, and other functions, based on the amount of space each uses.

In designing the company value stream income statement, the company decided to make visible two other business functions, product development and sales and marketing, that made up the majority of non-value stream costs. The expenses of all other business functions, such as accounting, human resources and information technology, are aggregated into general and administrative.

The horizontal format of this company value stream income statement aligns with a value stream organization, especially for making visible how the company operating profit (which is shown as "value stream profit") of

	OEM Value Stream	Systems Value Stream	New Product Development	Sales & Marketing	General & Administrative	Total
Sales	$ 1,039,440	$ 1,009,246				$ 2,048,686
Materials	424,763	339,810	84,953			849,526
Direct Labor	189,336	123,648				312,984
Machines	88,800	27,750				116,550
Outside Processing	36,000	17,731				53,731
Support Labor	87,662	67,616	40,772	93,315	53,056	342,421
Facilities	15,450	10,300	3,090	3,090	9,270	41,200
Other Costs	1,933	2,899	483	2,416	1,933	9,664
Total Costs	843,944	589,754	129,298	98,821	64,259	1,726,076
Value Stream Profit	$ 195,496	$ 419,492	$ (129,298)	$ (98,821)	$ (64,259)	$ 322,610
Return on Sales	19%	42%	-6%	-5%	-3%	16%

Beginning Inventory	1,186,035
Ending Inventory	963,148
Change in Inventory	$ (222,887)

Profit Before Tax	$ 99,723
Return on Sales	5%

FIGURE 6.2
Company Income Statement in Value Stream Format

$322,610 was generated. It is now clear that the two order fulfillment value streams must generate enough operating profit to "pay" for the other functional expenses of the business. This will become useful when calculating hurdle rates, which will be explained in Chapter 8.

The final step in developing a company value stream income statement is to segregate and make visible all "accounting adjustments" that are made for external reporting purposes to arrive at the net profit reported on the financial statements. The company in Figure 6.2 is a manufacturing company, and it must adjust the inventory value on the balance sheet each month, which is shown on the inventory adjustment line.

Segregating the accounting adjustments from operating profit makes visible the primary cause of the profit of $99,723. On this income statement, the decrease in inventory of $222,887 negatively impacted a solid operating profit of $322,610.

A company value stream income statement creates improved visibility into overall company financial performance. Operating profit, based on actual revenue and actual costs, reveals the true financial performance of business operations, and managers can be held responsible and accountable for improving operating profit. Segregating accounting adjustments "below the line" eliminates the confusion they cause for non-financial managers, who no longer have to try to explain something they don't understand.

WRAP UP

"Change the physical to change the financials" is a phrase I often use when working with companies to drive home the point that operational improvement must be the engine to drive financial improvement. This is why value stream income statements are an essential component of analysis and decision making in lean companies. When combined with the other two box score components – performance measurements and capacity – they create an analytical tool to learn about these cause–effect relationships, as illustrated in Figure 6.3.

"It's about spending, not costs" is the chapter title I used in the first edition of *The Lean CFO* for the chapter that explained value stream income statements and value stream costing. That title is another way to

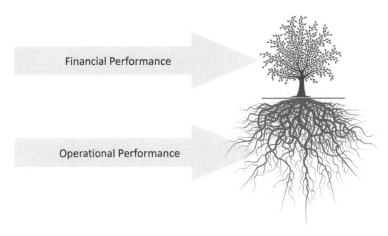

Financial Performance

Operational Performance

FIGURE 6.3
Drivers of Financial Performance

explain how to use value stream income statements. Any cost that appears on a financial statement is the result of a spending decision in a process, whether it be hiring an employee, buying supplies, or operational practices. Understanding the root causes of spending and improving methods of spending will ultimately manage costs.

Chapters 4, 5 and 6 explained how to build a box score. Now it's time to learn how to use box scores in lean companies in Chapters 7 and 8. Chapter 7 explains how box scores are integrated with lean practices to create a value stream management system to plan, improve, control and manage value streams. Chapter 8 explains how to incorporate box scores into analysis and decision making as it relates to understanding the profitability of decisions.

7

Value Stream Management

INTRODUCTION

Value stream management is the integration of lean management accounting with lean practices into a holistic management system. Value stream management is designed to serve customers better, improve productivity and improve financial performance.

A *value stream management system* is deployed at the *value stream or business process* level of a lean company and consists of the tools, practices and routines to control, improve, plan and manage any operational value stream or administrative business process. It can be deployed in any lean company, and in any type of industry.

Figure 7.1 illustrates the value stream management system. *Planning*, known as annual strategy deployment, is the engine that sets the improvement priorities for the company based on three to five initiatives that are expected to be completed in a year. *Improving* is based on the priorities and initiatives from strategy deployment and begins with value streams developing continuous improvement plans. The value streams manage their improvement activities in weekly value stream meetings. *Controlling* is based on daily lean management systems, deployed at the cell level, providing the necessary daily control to meet customer needs and identify problems and issues. *Managing* is based on manager standard work, coaching cycles and tiered meetings.

The best way to learn how lean management accounting is integrated with lean practices is to follow a company through the entire value stream management process. We are going to look at how Ross Manufacturing's leadership team uses strategy deployment; how one of its value streams, the Tube value stream, manages continuous improvement activities; how the machine cell in the Tube value streams uses daily lean management for

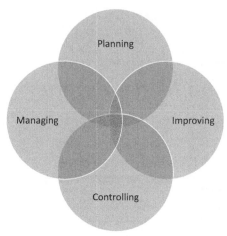

FIGURE 7.1
Value Stream Management System

control; and finally, how Ross's accounting team has integrated itself into the value stream management system.

PLANNING THE VALUE STREAM – STRATEGY DEPLOYMENT

The practice of strategy deployment is also known as Hoshin or Hoshin Kanri and it differs significantly from traditional planning processes. Strategy deployment focuses on actions to drive the numbers, not just what the numbers need to be. It focuses on a few annual objectives that are expected to be met in the coming year and is a collaborative process where senior leaders and managers agree on the actions. The strategy deployment process follows the PDCA cycle and is illustrated in Figure 7.2.

A tool which is often used in strategy deployment is the X-matrix which is illustrated in Figure 7.3. The X-matrix is a one-page document to summarize strategy deployment for a company, value stream or department. There are different versions of X-matrices, but all follow the general pattern of answering the basic questions, beginning on the left side of the matrix and moving in a clockwise direction:

- What are the few objectives? Annual objectives on the left side of the matrix.

FIGURE 7.2
Strategy Deployment Process

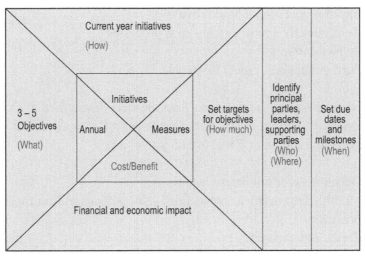

FIGURE 7.3
X-Matrix Example

- How will they be achieved? Current year initiatives on the top of the matrix.
- How much improvement is desired? Measurements on the right side of the matrix.
- Who, when, and where will the improvements be made are also listed on the right side of the matrix.
- The financial and operational benefits are listed on the bottom of the matrix.

Now let's look at how Ross Manufacturing's leadership team used an X-matrix to develop its strategy deployment plan for the year following the PDCA process illustrated in Figure 7.2.

The Plan Step

Using Figure 7.4 as a reference, let's review the Ross Manufacturing corporate X-matrix in a clockwise fashion beginning with annual objectives. Ross's five-year strategic plan is to leverage lean to create a competitive advantage in the marketplace. The leadership team has identified five specific annual objectives (the left side of Figure 7.4) for the upcoming year:

- Have the shortest lead times and highest on-time delivery in the industry.
- Improve operational productivity.
- Continuously improve all business processes.
- Reduce costs.
- Further enhance respect for people.

Based on these annual objectives Ross's leaders determined five current year company initiatives that will form the basis for improvement events throughout the company. These five initiatives are:

- Decrease order fulfillment lead times.
- Monthly improvement events in all value streams and administrative processes.
- Create 20% capacity.
- Implement pull systems in all value streams.
- Decrease safety incidents.

Ross's leadership team uses its company lean performance measurements (developed using the Linkage Chart process described in Chapter 4) to set the improvement targets desired for the upcoming year:

- 20% improvement in sales growth, lead times, delivery and productivity.

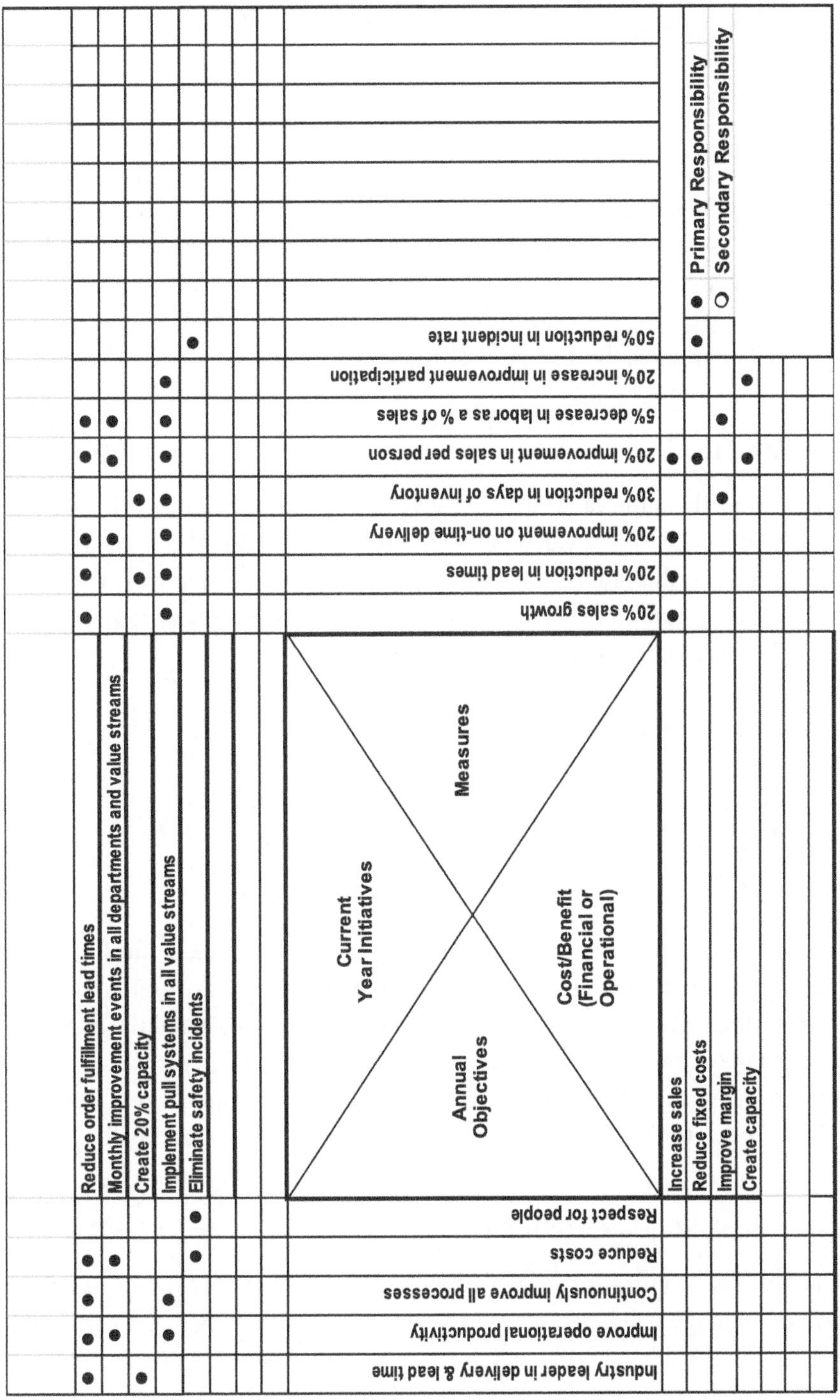

Current Year Initiatives

Measures

Annual Objectives

Cost/Benefit (Financial or Operational)

Current Year Initiatives:
- Reduce order fulfillment lead times
- Monthly improvement events in all departments and value streams
- Create 20% capacity
- Implement pull systems in all value streams
- Eliminate safety incidents

Measures:
- 20% sales growth
- 20% reduction in lead times
- 20% improvement on on-time delivery
- 30% reduction in days of inventory
- 20% improvement in sales per person
- 5% decrease in labor as a % of sales
- 20% increase in improvement participation
- 50% reduction in incident rate

Annual Objectives:
- Industry leader in delivery & lead time
- Improve operational productivity
- Continuously improve all processes
- Reduce costs
- Respect for people

Cost/Benefit (Financial or Operational):
- Increase sales
- Reduce fixed costs
- Improve margin
- Create capacity

● Primary Responsibility
○ Secondary Responsibility

FIGURE 7.4
Ross Manufacturing Company X-Matrix

- 5% decrease in labor expense as a percentage of sales.
- 30% reduction in days of inventory.
- 50% reduction in safety incident rate.

After completing the company X-matrix, Ross's leaders will meet with each of their value stream managers to review the document. After that meeting, as part of the "do step" in the strategy deployment process, each value stream will develop its own X-matrix to align with the company X-matrix. We will now look at how Ross's Tube value stream developed its X-matrix based on the company X-matrix.

The Do Step

In this step, the Tube value stream uses the company current year initiatives, from Figure 7.4, as its value stream annual objectives (the left side of its X-matrix), as illustrated in Figure 7.5. Using these objectives, the Tube value stream team identifies five areas of operational improvement to complete in the coming year (the top of Figure 7.5):

- Improve quality and rework.
- Implement single piece flow.
- Reduce inventory.
- Implement point-of-use delivery from top suppliers.
- Implement safety training and audits.

Like Ross's leadership, the Tube value stream's lean performance measurements were derived from the Linkage Chart and are used in their X-matrix (the right side of Figure 7.5). When the team projected the expected percentage of improvement for its value stream performance measurements, they realized they differed a bit from the company's improvement targets. This takes us to the next step of strategy deployment, the catchball process.

The Check Step – Catchball

Catchball is a communication process where company leadership and value stream managers discuss initiatives, targets and resources to get consensus on the few, critical actions which must be completed to achieve company goals. Catchball is the opposite of traditional top-down management in

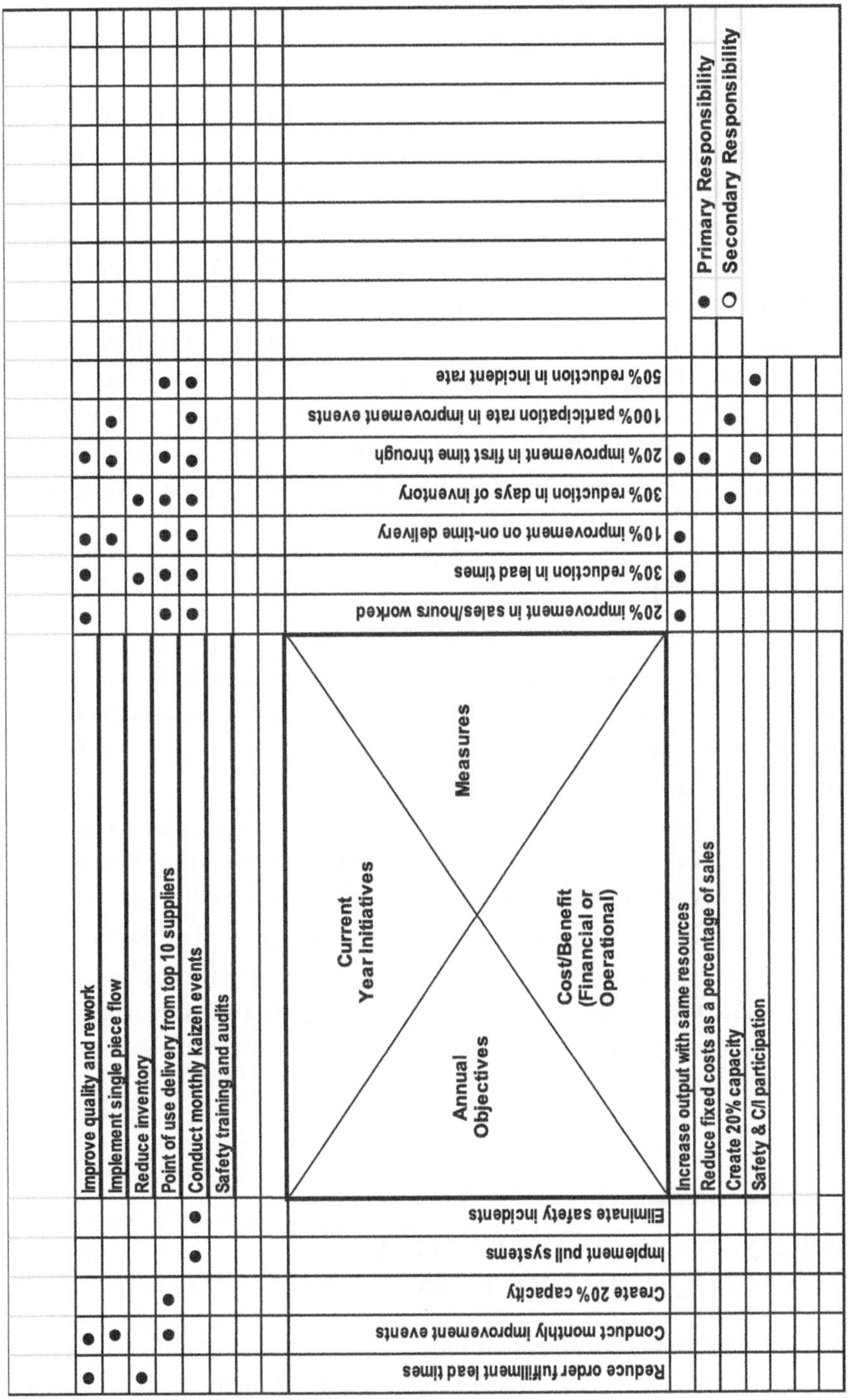

Current Year Initiatives

- Improve quality and rework
- Implement single piece flow
- Reduce inventory
- Point of use delivery from top 10 suppliers
- Conduct monthly kaizen events
- Safety training and audits

Annual Objectives

- Reduce order fulfillment lead times
- Conduct monthly improvement events
- Create 20% capacity
- Implement pull systems
- Eliminate safety incidents

Measures

- 20% improvement in sales/hours worked
- 30% reduction in lead times
- 10% improvement on on-time delivery
- 30% reduction in days of inventory
- 20% improvement in first time through
- 100% participation rate in improvement events
- 50% reduction in incident rate

Cost/Benefit (Financial or Operational)

- Increase output with same resources
- Reduce fixed costs as a percentage of sales
- Create 20% capacity
- Safety & CI participation

● Primary Responsibility
○ Secondary Responsibility

FIGURE 7.5
Tube Value Stream X-Matrix

that managers and leaders work together to agree in advance about what level of improvement managers are committing to, as opposed to top management dictating targets.

Looking at the Tube value stream X-matrix in Figure 7.5, the Tube value stream has committed to improvement targets in line with the company X-matrix in productivity (sales per hours worked), inventory reduction, safety and quality.

The Tube value stream team believes it can achieve a 30% reduction in lead time, rather than 20%, but can only commit to a 10% improvement in on-time delivery because its current on-time delivery is quite high.

It believes it can get to a 100% improvement event participation rate because the entire value stream team is very enthusiastic about lean. After discussion between the Tube value stream manager and the Ross leadership team, there is mutual agreement to these targets for the Tube value stream.

The Adjust Step

There are two outcomes in the adjust step in strategy deployment. The first is that X-matrices can be revised as a result of catchball. If there is consensus between the leadership team and the value streams, then the second outcome that can happen in the adjust step is that action plans for the year can be finalized.

For the company initiatives, Ross's leadership team identifies one of its members to be the sponsor of each initiative. The responsibility of each sponsor is to coordinate the improvement activities of all the value streams and measure progress using the company performance measurements.

The overriding goal of strategy deployment is to align the improvement activities in a lean company around the company's annual objectives and initiatives. Now let's look at how the Tube value stream manages improving its value stream.

IMPROVING THE VALUE STREAM – CONTINUOUS IMPROVEMENT

As explained in Chapter 3, continuous improvement is not random, haphazard or dictated by top management in lean companies. It is done by the people who work in the process and managed by value stream teams. Company leadership outlines the annual objectives in strategy deployment, and then it is up to value stream teams to determine the specific improvements to be made to achieve their annual improvement targets.

In lean companies, the planning and conducting of improvement activities follows the process as illustrated in Figure 7.6. The structured approach of following this process focuses on creating a new, improved and sustained standard of performance through:

- Kaizen events, which are planned, multi-day events designed to achieve breakthrough change and derived through strategy deployment.
- Value stream improvement events, which are identified using value stream performance measurements. These improvement activities are identified in the weekly value stream team meeting and can be conducted as part of the value stream team's regular work.

Now let's follow the Ross Manufacturing's Tube value stream as it plans and manages its continuous improvement activities, following the process summarized in Figure 7.6.

FIGURE 7.6
Improving the Value Stream

Planning the Improvements

Planning the improvements for the Tube value stream team begins with creating a future state value stream map. Developing a future state map is a design process, meaning the future state map is designed to achieve a level of improved performance based on these value stream performance measurements in the Tube value stream X-matrix. Using its current state box score, as illustrated in Figure 7.7, the team projects the future state value stream performance measurements:

- The first time through rate must improve from 58.3% to 70%. When designing the future state, each cell will have to be reviewed to determine their reduction in scrap rates.
- Reducing days of inventory from 29.25 to 20.48 focuses the team on how much work-in-process inventory must be reduced in the future state.

Performance Measurements	Current State	Target Improvement	Target Future State
Productivity	$ 27,797	20%	$ 33,356
Delivery	81%	10%	89%
Cost	$ 207	$ -	$ 207
Quality	58.3%	20%	70.0%
Days Inventory	29.25	30%	20.48
Average Lead Time	10.78	30%	7.54
Capacity			
Productive	64.90%		
Nonproductive	42.64%		
Available	-7.54%		
Income Statement			
Revenue	861,696		
Materials	292,516		
Contribution Margin	569,180		
Direct Costs	127,484		
Shared Costs	29,527		
Total Production Costs	157,011		
Value Stream Operating Profit	412,169		
	47.8%		

FIGURE 7.7
Current State Box Score

- The future state measurements of a 7.54-day lead time and 89% on-time delivery will help the team to determine which lean operating practices must be in place to create flow.

Using the current state map (Figure 7.8) as a baseline, the team designs a future state value stream map, as illustrated in Figure 7.9, that will have improved quality, less inventory, a shorter lead time and improved on-time delivery. Comparing the future state map to the current state map, the team identifies the following improvements:

- Reducing scrap and rework in the machine and welding cells, through a series of monthly improvement events.
- Design and implement a pull system using single piece flow, which is explained in Figure 7.9.

The final step in mapping the future state of the value stream is to update the future state box score, as shown in Figure 7.10. The purpose of creating a future state box score is to inform Ross's leadership of the expected improvements in both operating and financial performance. The future state box score reveals the actual impact of the planned kaizen events:

- The improvement in all performance measurements exceeds the targets set during strategy deployment.
- About 20% capacity (from -7.54% to 14.61%) will be created due to the kaizen events which will allow the value stream to meet an expected increase in demand and increase revenue.
- The improvements in quality and days of inventory will reduce actual material costs.
- The freed-up capacity will allow the value stream to decrease overtime costs, which reduces direct costs.

The benefit of using box scores in future state mapping events is that it makes the mapping event a data-driven process rather than a "hope-for" process. The planned kaizen events *will achieve* the performance improvements desired in strategy deployment. Now it's just a matter of conducting the events.

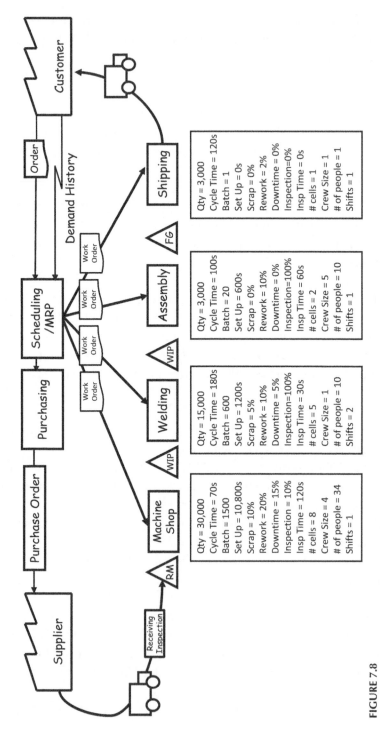

FIGURE 7.8
Tube Current State Value Stream Map

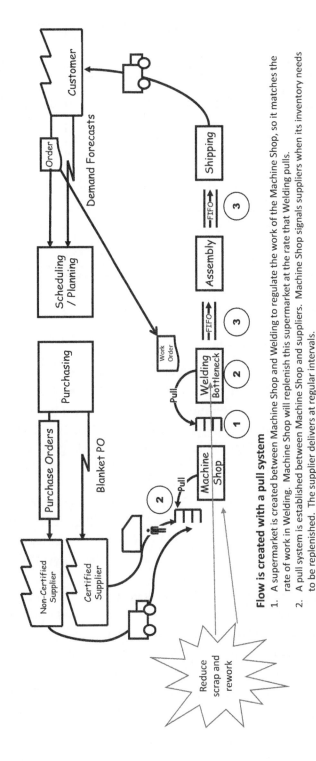

Flow is created with a pull system

1. A supermarket is created between Machine Shop and Welding to regulate the work of the Machine Shop, so it matches the rate of work in Welding. Machine Shop will replenish this supermarket at the rate that Welding pulls.

2. A pull system is established between Machine Shop and suppliers. Machine Shop signals suppliers when its inventory needs to be replenished. The supplier delivers at regular intervals.

3. Because Assembly works faster than Welding, it produces one-at-a time as Welding completes its work. Then the finished product flows directly to Shipping for delivery to the customer.

The result: Decrease in days of inventory and reduction in lead time

FIGURE 7.9
Tube Value Stream Future State Map

Performance Measurements	Current State	Target Improvement	Target Future State		Future State Map	Actual Improvement
Productivity	$ 27,797	20%	$ 33,356		$ 34,490	24%
Delivery	81%	10%	89%		100%	24%
Cost	$ 207	$ -	$ 207		$ 130	-37%
Quality	58.3%	20%	70.0%		78.6%	35%
Days Inventory	29.25	30%	20.48		20.48	-30%
Average Lead Time	10.78	30%	7.54		5.39	-50%
Capacity						
Productive	64.90%				64.90%	
Nonproductive	42.64%				20.49%	
Available	-7.54%				14.61%	
Income Statement						
Revenue	861,696				1,069,200	
Materials	292,516				204,761	
Contribution Margin	569,180				864,439	
Direct Costs	127,484				117,233	
Shared Costs	29,527				29,528	
Total Production Costs	157,011				146,761	
Value Stream Operating Profit	412,169				717,678	
	47.8%				67.1%	

FIGURE 7.10
Future State Box Score

Do – Conducting Kaizen Events

Over the years I have been asked to facilitate multi-day kaizen events. In all cases I followed a structured agenda based on the PDCA process. Fully explaining the details of how to conduct a kaizen event would be beyond the scope of this book. If you would like to learn more about conducting kaizen events following the PDCA process, there are many good books available, such as *The Kaizen Event Planner* by Karen Martin and *Kaizen Sketchbook* by Marypat Cooper.

What is important to discuss here, is how to integrate box scores and other relevant information into each kaizen event. This is illustrated by the sample A-3 for a kaizen event, as illustrated in Figure 7.11. For each kaizen event, the Tube value stream team must gather and use the following data:

- Box 2: Gather preliminary data, using components of the box score and relevant event-specific information, to measure *the extent* of the problem in planning the event. This data will be finalized during the event.
- Box 3: During the event, project future improvement targets using the same data as used in box 2.
- Box 6: Measure the effectiveness of solutions using the data from boxes 2 and 3.

1. Problem/Issue/Opportunity

Define the problem

2. Current State

Measure the extent of the problem:
- *current state box score*
- *data specific to the problem statement*

3. Future State

Project improvement targets for the event based on data in current state box score and other specific data

4. Root Cause Analysis

Root cause analysis related to problem, issue or business case. Identify information issues.

5. Solution Ideas

Define or brainstorm solutions to eliminate/mitigate root causes.

6. Rapid Experiments

Use data from boxes 2 & 3 to measure the impact of solutions being tested

7. Completion Plan

Use data to determine the best solution to implement

8. New Standard Work

Define new standard work to sustain the improvements

9. Insights & Follow up

In value stream weekly meetings, use weekly box scores to measure sustainment of improvements

FIGURE 7.11
Using Box Scores in Kaizen Events

- Box 7: Use the data from the testing of solutions to determine the improvements to implement.
- Box 9: Use the actual weekly value stream box scores in the weekly meeting to evaluate if the improvements have been sustained.

Check and Adjust – the Weekly Value Stream Team Meeting

The Tube value stream team has overall responsibility and accountability for the operating and financial performance of the value stream. The team members are made up of a value stream manager, operational managers and functional subject matter experts such as quality, engineering, sales and accounting.

The purpose of the weekly value stream team meeting is to manage the value stream towards its improvement targets by reviewing actual operating performance and the impact of all improvement events. The team conducts a weekly 30-minute meeting around the value stream visual board (Figure 7.12), and the format of the board drives the agenda for the weekly meeting.

The top row of the board shows the trend of each performance measurement using a simple line graph, plotting actual performance against the quarterly target. As the team reviews each measurement it performs a

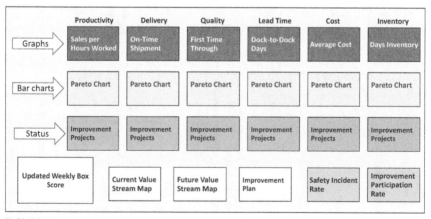

FIGURE 7.12
Tube Value Stream Visual Board

verbal root cause analysis to determine causes of both good and poor performance. The causes of poor operating performance are used to update the Pareto charts in the second row of the board.

Next, the team reviews the status of all active improvement activities and provides updates. They assess actual results of all completed improvement events and their impact on performance.

The adjust step in the weekly value stream meeting focuses on synthesizing all this information in relation to overall value stream performance as shown in the weekly box score (Figure 7.13). The output of the adjust step can consist of any of the following:

- A short-term operating action plan of countermeasures that focuses on reacting to current operating conditions to better manage the flow of orders.
- Adjusting the value stream improvement plan to eliminate the primary root causes of poor performance.
- Escalating recurring problems and issues to the leadership team so it can remove roadblocks or provide the necessary resources to the Tube value stream team to improve performance.

In the weekly meeting, using the weekly box score numbers makes it easier for the Tube value stream team to:

- Identify the primary root causes of poor operating performance.
- Better understand the relationships between operating and financial performance trends.
- Make the necessary adjustments to "get back on track."

The weekly value stream team meeting is also a communication tool for Ross's leadership team. They are required to attend value stream team meetings at least twice a month, as observers, to learn firsthand the current trends in operating and financial performance rather than waiting on the month-end financial statements.

Now let's review daily lean management, which is the cornerstone to controlling the value stream.

	WEEKLY NUMBERS	7-Jan	14-Jan	21-Jan	28-Jan	4-Feb	11-Feb	18-Feb	25-Feb	4-Mar	11-Mar	18-Mar	25-Mar	1-Apr	Goal
Value Stream Performance Measurements	Productivity ($/person)	$5,562	$4,762	$5,882	$6,356	$5,730	$6,142	$5,527							$5,800
	On Time Shipment	82%	92%	81%	82%	85%	89%	92%							96%
	Inventory Days	14	18	12	19	16	14	12							10
	First Pass Quality	88%	78%	85%	73%	85%	88%	88%							95%
	Average Product Cost	$15.83	$16.94	$15.81	$16.13	$15.76	$15.46	$15.71							$14.86
	Employee Engagement	28%	28%	28%	35%	35%	35%	35%							42%
Value Stream Capacity	Productive Time %	69%	59%	73%	68%	62%	66%	59%							60%
	Non-Productive Time %	32%	27%	34%	32%	29%	31%	28%							28%
	Available Time %	-1%	13%	-7%	0%	10%	3%	13%							12%
Value Stream Financials	REVENUE	$339,292	$280,978	$358,794	$451,272	$406,801	$436,071	$392,411							$464,000
	Materials	$169,220	$152,649	$183,740	$213,730	$180,125	$188,048	$169,220							$180,390
	Labor Costs	$77,003	$62,241	$78,066	$80,044	$74,901	$81,758	$74,901							$84,395
	Machine Cost	$14,321	$14,321	$14,321	$14,321	$14,321	$14,321	$14,321							$14,321
	Other Costs	$17,887	$17,563	$17,995	$18,170	$17,956	$18,097	$17,887							$18,146
	PROFIT	$60,861	$34,204	$64,672	$125,007	$119,498	$133,847	$116,081							$166,748
	Return on Revenue	18%	12%	18%	28%	29%	31%	30%							36%
28%	Hurdle Rate	-10%	-16%	-10%	0%	1%	3%	2%							8%

FIGURE 7.13

Tube Value Stream Weekly Box Score

CONTROLLING – DAILY LEAN MANAGEMENT

Daily lean management practices create a standard cadence of activities in cells to control the work, serve customers, identify problems, and trouble-shoot problems as they occur. Daily lean management is the opposite of traditional business firefighting, where employees are continually moving from problem to problem but never really solving the problems. Daily lean management becomes the daily work routine for the employees in a cell.

Daily lean management also follows the PDCA process, as illustrated in Figure 7.14, and is designed to reveal the underlying causes of perform-ance issues in four primary areas, all related to serving customers:

- Quality – is a process step capable of producing the same result every time?
- Availability – is a process step able to perform when needed?
- Capacity – is a process step capacity adequate to perform when it needs to perform?
- Flexible – is a process step flexible to changing conditions?

Let's follow how the machine work cell in the Tube value stream set up their daily lean management system as they build their visual performance board, which is illustrated in Figure 7.15, and develop an agenda for their daily huddle.

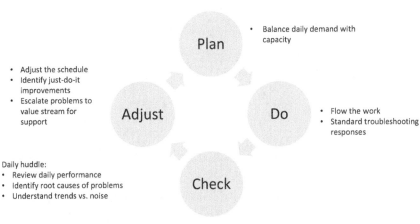

FIGURE 7.14
Daily Lean Management Process

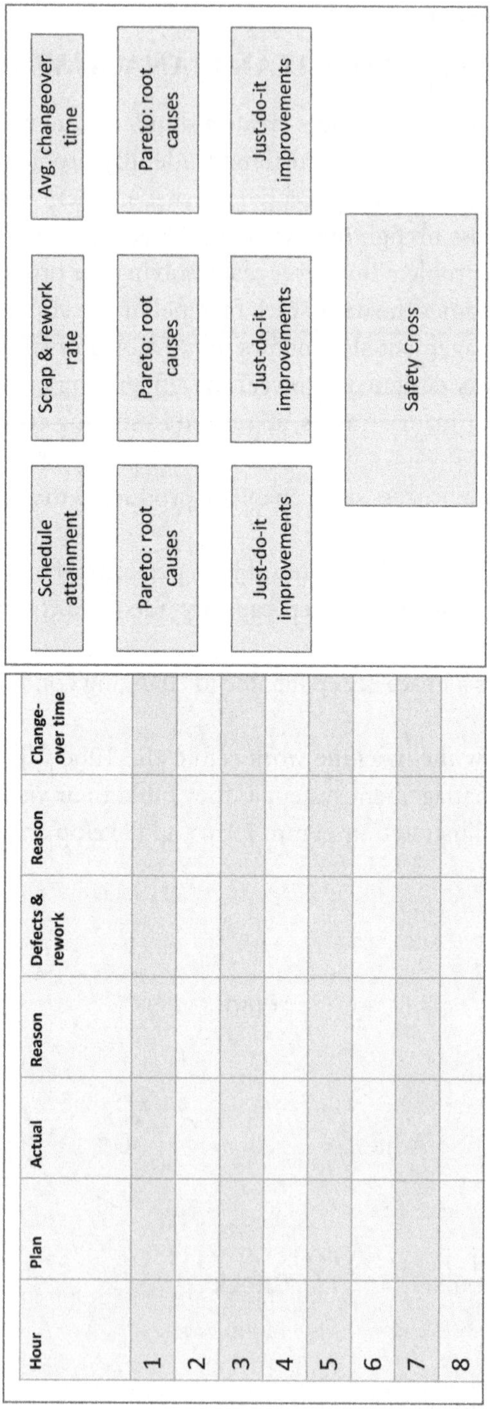

PLAN & DO: Daily Schedule & Status

Hour	Plan	Actual	Reason	Defects & rework	Reason	Change-over time
1						
2						
3						
4						
5						
6						
7						
8						

CHECK & ADJUST: Measurements and Actions

Schedule attainment	Scrap & rework rate	Avg. changeover time
Pareto: root causes	Pareto: root causes	Pareto: root causes
Just-do-it improvements	Just-do-it improvements	Just-do-it improvements

Safety Cross

FIGURE 7.15
The Visual Board

The initial step for the machine cell team is to determine its daily lean performance measurements, which need to be aligned with strategy deployment. Using the Tube value stream X-matrix and value stream map, the machine cell team selects the following lean performance measurements:

- Schedule attainment – to understand the reasons it does not meet daily demand.
- Kanban levels – the implementation of the pull system will include standard levels of work-in-process inventory levels in the cell. Changes in kanban levels indicate issues with flow and the team will monitor these changes visually.
- Scrap and rework rate – the Tube value stream plans to improve quality and measuring scrap and rework in the machine cell will provide the necessary root causes to plan improvements and measure their impact.
- Changeover time – in order to reduce value stream lead time and improve delivery, the machine cell must focus on understanding the underlying causes of its changeover times.
- Safety incidents – safety incidents will be measured daily using a safety cross.

All of these daily lean performance measurements will be recorded on the visual board, with the exception of kanban levels, which will be monitored visually during the workday.

Plan and Do – the Daily Schedule and Executing the Work

The plan step in daily lean management is to determine exactly what work can be completed in the day, which requires balancing demand with the available capacity. The cell team will use machine hours to determine available capacity.

The machine cell data box on the current state value stream map (Figure 7.8) gives the team the information to calculate available capacity, based on 80% of total capacity, as follows:

- 8 machines x one 8-hour shift = 64 total daily machine hours
- 80% of 64 total hours = 51 available hours to schedule

Using 51 available hours per day, the team will calculate its plan each day in terms of the number of units to be completed in the 51 hours.

Next, the team must determine how to schedule the day and how often to "check" actual to the schedule. Given that the average cycle time of the machines is 70 seconds, the team determines it would be best to schedule and measure "day by the hour," which is shown in the illustration of the daily board in Figure 7.15.

By checking actual production against an hourly schedule, the team will be able to understand and document current problems and make the necessary schedule adjustments to catch up if production falls behind. The team will use the "reason" column in the daily schedule to record why actual hourly production does not meet plan.

In order to understand scrap and rework, it will be also measured on an hourly basis and the reasons will be recorded on the daily board. Actual changeover time will be recorded when one occurs. This "day by the hour" plan and status check will allow the cell team to respond with troubleshooting to any abnormal conditions as they occur.

Check and Adjust – the Daily Huddle

Because the machine cell works one shift, the team decides to hold its daily huddle around the visual board at the end of the shift. This will allow them to review the current day and set the plan for the next day, especially if schedule attainment was not achieved.

Prior to the huddle, the performance measurements on the board are updated – schedule attainment, scrap/rework, average changeover time. These measures are presented in the format of a process control chart, as illustrated in Figure 7.16. Actual performance is plotted against average performance, which is based on historical information. Safety is recorded on a 20-working-day safety cross with green indicating no incidents and red indicating an incident.

During the huddle, the team reviews each process control chart to identify negative trends, which are considered two or more days below the average. In cases of negative trends, an initial root cause analysis is done during the meeting and specific actions, in the form of just-do-it improvements, are scheduled. In cases where recurring problems cannot be solved by the machine cell team, they escalate the problem to the Tube value stream team. As shown in Figure 7.15 both the root causes and improvements related to each performance measurement are documented on the visual board.

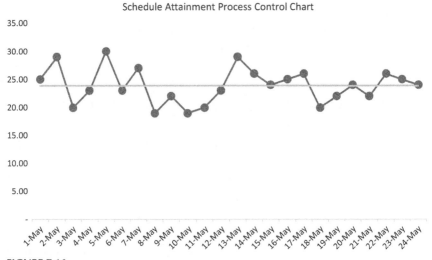

FIGURE 7.16
Schedule Attainment Process Control Chart

The cycle of daily lean management is conducive to learning about root causes of operating performance through the use of relevant daily lean performance measures. It's much easier to identify gaps from standard levels of performance and their root causes on a daily basis than a longer time frame.

A final note about daily lean management. Setting up daily lean management should be based on how fast a cell or process needs to identify and respond to changing conditions and how long it takes for countermeasures to be reflected in process performance.

In the case of the machine cell, it used a "day-by-the-hour" plan and status check because of its short cycle times. In cells and processes with longer cycle times, such as services or knowledge-based work, it may be more relevant to set up cadences such as day-by-the-day or week-by-the day.

MANAGING – ACCOUNTING'S ROLE IN VALUE STREAM MANAGEMENT

The numbers of lean management accounting – performance measurements and box scores – are the relevant and reliable information needed in lean companies, but they are simply tools which must be used properly to be effective. Integrating the numbers into standard lean practices such as strategy deployment, improvement activities and daily lean management requires foresight and leadership from accounting.

Ross's accounting team integrated itself into the value stream management practices to achieve two objectives: (1) to learn about the cause–effect relationships between operating practices and financial performance, and (2) to provide the necessary coaching to help everyone else learn how to use the numbers. Here are the specific practices the accounting team employs:

- Each cost accounting manager is assigned to two value stream teams. They attend all weekly meetings and respond to periodic analytical requests. Each value stream team knows exactly which person in accounting to contact for rapid assistance.
- An accounting team member is part of planned kaizen event teams or available as a subject matter expert during events. Accounting team members are selected for kaizen teams based on how their work relates to the process being studied in the kaizen event.
- Each accounting team member has a regular schedule of daily huddles to attend and observe. The huddle schedule is rotated periodically so all team members are exposed to all daily huddles being conducted in Ross.
- Accounting is included in the escalation of problems and issues when financial performance may be impacted.
- Each accounting team member has a Gemba walk schedule. They "go to the Gemba" regularly to visually see operations in action and engage with people on problems and issues they are facing. Like the daily huddle schedule, the Gemba walk schedule is rotated periodically.

WRAP UP: VALUE STREAM MANAGEMENT

As part of a lean management accounting transformation, it is essential to integrate the numbers of lean management accounting into all lean practices to improve the quality of the numerous decisions which are made in strategy deployment, daily lean management and continuous improvement activities. It's also important to also integrate the accounting team because they can provide the required analytical skills to establish the true cause–effect relationships between lean operating performance and financial performance.

It's best to approach lean management accounting and lean practices such as strategy deployment, continuous improvement and daily lean management as one holistic system rather than separate systems.

In the next chapter, we will look at integrating lean management accounting into the analytical and decision-making processes of lean companies.

8

Lean Decision Making

BOX SCORE THINKING

In lean management accounting, the box score is the relevant and reliable information designed to improve the quality of decision making, as illustrated in Figure 8.1. The box score provides decision makers with information that is understandable in lean companies and is useful in all types of decisions. Box scores are based on actual information which is both verifiable and valid.

The numbers and relationships in a box score make visible the true relationships between lean operating performance and financial performance. This drives changes in the thinking habits of decision makers. The box score components require decision makers to consider the overall economic impact of a decision both operationally and financially, which is summarized in Figure 8.2.

USE THE PDCA PROCESS

Another element of lean decision making is using the PDCA process, as explained in Chapter 3, as the standard work to follow when performing an analysis. Any business decision is an attempt to solve a problem. It may be a gap from standard problem, where financial performance is below expectations, or it could be solving the problem of how to achieve an improved and sustained level of financial performance in the future. PDCA can be applied to decision making to:

- Compare a current state box score to a future state box score.
- Consider the total incremental change to the box score over the time frame of the decision.
- Identify the root causes which must be removed for the decision to achieve the future state.

Using a box score with the PDCA process creates a standardized approach to decision making that can be applied to all functions in a lean company. Let's now look at how some companies use box scores and the PDCA process in lean decision making.

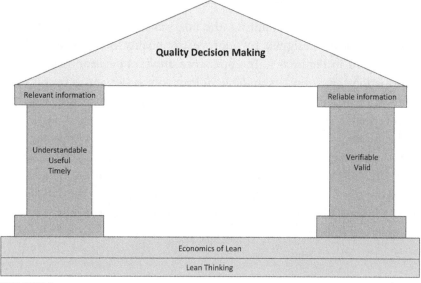

FIGURE 8.1
Quality Decision Making

Determine changes in sales

Determine changes in actual fixed costs

Determine changes in variable costs and margin

Determine the impact on capacity

Determine the impact on performance

Determine the impact on cash

FIGURE 8.2
Box Score Visibility

INCREASING CAPACITY TO MEET DEMAND

Payroll Providers, Inc. is a locally owned company, with 15 employees, that provides payroll services to local small and medium-size companies. Margaret, the owner of the company, previously worked as director of human resources for a larger company whose strategy was based on lean thinking. When Margaret started Payroll Providers, lean practices were incorporated into all aspects of work, including using a box score and a weekly improvement meeting.

In this week's meeting, Margaret displays the current state box score (Figure 8.3, column A) and explains, based on projected client increases in headcount and Payroll Providers adding new clients, that the 7% available capacity is not enough to meet this increase in demand. Currently they process payroll for 4,875 employees per month and this is expected to increase by 23% to 6,000 employees per month.

Payroll Providers, Inc.	A Current State	B Future State Hire People	C Future State Continuous Improvement
Performance Measurements			
Productivity	$ 11,375	$ 10,500	$ 14,000
Average Cost per Unit	$ 31.86	$ 31.92	$ 28.53
Quality (Defect Rate)	20.0%	20.0%	15.0%
Average Flow Time (hours)	8.2	6.67	6.67
Capacity			
Productive	36%	33%	44%
Nonproductive	52%	50%	38%
Continuous Improvement	5%	5%	5%
Available	7%	11%	12%
Income Statement			
Revenue	170,625	210,000	210,000
Software Subscription Fees	99,938	123,000	123,000
Contribution Margin	70,688	87,000	87,000
Value Stream Costs			
Labor	39,375	52,500	39,375
Other Operating Expenses	16,025	16,025	16,025
Total Costs	55,400	68,525	55,400
Value Stream Operating Profit	15,288	18,475	31,600
Return on Sales	9.0%	8.8%	18.5%

FIGURE 8.3
Increasing Capacity to Meet Demand

Margaret also prepared a future state box score based on hiring an additional five employees to meet demand (Figure 8.3, column B). She explained that Payroll Providers' profit would improve from $15,288 per month to $18,475 per month, but its return on sales would go down to 8.8%. The team did not like the return on sales decreasing because their incentive program increases employee bonuses when the company achieves a 10% return on sales.

The team asked if she would allow them one week to come up with some improvement activities that could create enough capacity to avoid hiring additional employees. The team then reviewed what made up the 52% of non-productive capacity in detail, and identified on three forms of waste:

- 20% defect rate of information received from client companies that must be corrected before processing.
- 30% of their time is spent in a variety of reviewing and checking activities, some of which is due to the defect rate.
- 20% of time is spent on other non-value added activities that prevent the team from processing payroll.

The team took a week to brainstorm some improvement activities and in next week's meeting they presented A-3 reports outlining improvements that can be completed over the next two months to reduce waste, as follows:

- Defect rate from 20% to 10%.
- Checking and reviewing from 30% to 20%.
- Other non-value added activities from 20% to 10%.

Margaret entered the updated waste data into her capacity calculator and produced a future state box score based on the improvements (Figure 8.3, column C). She explained to the team that the planned improvement activities would create more than enough capacity for the expected increase in demand and more than double monthly operating profit. They would also provide a cushion of 18% available capacity to meet longer-term increases in demand. Additionally, these improvements would be beneficial operationally, as indicated by improved performance in productivity, cost, quality and flow time.

Margaret used this as a learning opportunity. Even though she had the experience to make the decision herself, she decided to let the people who do the work solve the problem. The lessons learned when the people who do the work solve the problem stay with those people. In this case the team learned it is more beneficial financially to create capacity through continuous improvement rather than buying more capacity.

MAKE OR BUY DECISION

Joe, a Neutralia Company salesperson, was having a sales call meeting with Karen, the purchasing manager of Axent, a potential new customer. Karen expressed an interest in a monthly order of 3,000 Pro-Valve 602s beginning in three months. Joe quoted the list price of $50 per unit, which had been calculated based on a required 15% margin on the Pro-Valve 602 standard cost of $42.34. Karen thanked Joe for the quote and said she would get back to him. Two days later, Karen called Joe and explained that the $50 price was too high for Axent and that Axent's maximum price was $45 per unit. Joe, not wanting to lose the sale, and a new customer, let Karen know that he would get back to her.

Knowing Neutralia required a minimum of 15% margin on all sales, Joe thought that he would have to turn down the opportunity because the $45 sales price would only yield a margin of 5.92%, as illustrated in Figure 8.4. Because Joe really wanted to make this sale he decided to contact Neutralia's supply chain manager, Luis, in an effort to find a way to lower the cost of the product to achieve the required 15% margin at a $45 sales price.

Profitability Using Standard Cost		
		Quantity
Price	$45.00	3,000
Standard Cost	$42.34	
Profit per Unit	$2.66	
Margin Percentage	5.92%	
Take the Order?	NO	

FIGURE 8.4
Profitability Using Standard Costing

Low Cost Country Outsourcing		
		Quantity
Price	$45.00	3,000
Outsource Cost	$33.00	
Outsource Overhead %	7.50%	
Outsource Overhead Cost	$2.48	
Total Cost	$35.48	
Profit per Unit	$9.53	
Margin Percentage	21.17%	
Take the Order?	YES	

FIGURE 8.5
Profitability Using Outsourcing

Luis did some research and explained to Joe that the supplier of the raw materials would not agree to any purchase price discounts, but that he had found a supplier who could produce Pro-Valve 602s for a lower price than Neutralia's standard cost. The supplier quoted a landed cost of $33.00 per unit for Pro-Valve 602s. Joe ran the numbers, as shown in Figure 8.5, and the unit margin percentage for this order was now 21.17%, which was above the 15% minimum required margin. Joe was excited to close the deal with Axent and asked Luis to begin getting the new supplier set up. Luis explained that before he would do this, he wanted Joe to contact Sanja, the Pro-Valve value stream manager, to take another look at making this Pro-Valve 602 order in-house by analyzing it using a lean accounting box score.

Joe set up a meeting to talk with Sanja about this opportunity. Joe explained that the price Karen was willing to pay would not achieve the required 15% unit margin, and Luis had found a supplier who could make the product for a price that would achieve a 21.17% unit margin.

Sanja showed Joe his current state value stream box score, as shown in column 1 of Figure 8.6, and explained that with 6% available capacity, he did not have enough capacity to produce an additional 3,000 units per month. He asked Joe to give him a couple of days to work up future state box scores based on outsourcing and making in-house by purchasing more capacity.

Joe and Sanja met two days later and Sanja displayed the Pro-Valve box score on the conference room screen with two future states – outsourcing and making in-house. Using column 2 of Figure 8.6 as a reference, Sanja

Pro-Valve Value Stream Box Score	1 Current State	2 Future State Outsource	3 Future State In-house
Performance Measurements			
Productivity	$ 23,087	$ 25,301	$ 28,451
Delivery	82%	78%	86%
Average Cost per Unit	$ 15.97	$ 16.74	$ 17.44
Quality (First Pass Rate)	88.0%	82.0%	92.0%
Days Inventory	14	28	14
Capacity			
Productive	62%	62%	68%
Nonproductive	32%	32%	20%
Available	6%	6%	12%
Income Statement			
Revenue	1,408,333	1,543,333	1,543,333
Material Cost	765,000	871,425	817,500
Contribution Margin	643,333	671,908	725,833
Value Stream Costs			
Labor	267,083	267,083	276,559
Machines	59,433	59,433	62,500
Other Operating Expenses	74,233	74,233	74,233
Total Costs	400,749	400,749	413,292
Value Stream Operating Profit	242,584	271,159	312,541
Return on Sales	17.2%	17.6%	20.3%

FIGURE 8.6
Pro-Valve Value Stream Box Score

explained that while outsourcing would increase value stream profitability by almost $30,000 per month, it would also negatively impact value stream operating performance. Inconsistent supplier delivery would negatively impact on-time delivery and force the value stream to stock inventory. The supplier's quality was also lower than the quality the value stream produced.

Sanja then directed Joe to look at the third column on the box score (column 3 of Figure 8.6). He explained to Joe that by purchasing two new machines and hiring two new operators, the value stream could produce the additional 3,000 units per month, and value stream profitability would be $312,541 per month versus the $271,159 per month from outsourcing. Sanja also explained the operational benefits of the new machines – improved productivity and better quality.

Joe agreed with Sanja's evaluation. Sanja explained that the next step was for him and Joe to meet with Lois, the CFO, for final approval of buying the machines and hiring the operators. Joe was delighted because he could now take the order at Karen's desired price of $45.00 per unit and earn an excellent sales commission.

Joe learned that by using a box score, he gained a complete picture of each alternative in a make or buy decision. He learned a quality decision was based on much more than a standard margin percentage. It was based on improving operating performance and financial performance simultaneously.

PRICING AND QUOTING DECISIONS

Any company that sells products or services must set prices, which can be published list prices or quoted prices. However, customers ultimately decide prices based on the value they perceive they are receiving. In the case of list prices, such as a restaurant menu, customers may choose not to eat at a specific restaurant if they consider the prices too high for the value received. In the case of quoted prices, customers may simply reject the quote or attempt to negotiate a lower price.

Many factors, beyond the scope of this book, go into setting prices. But there are two common points of analysis in all price-setting activities:

- Calculating a desired price to charge to earn a desired profit.
- Calculating the profitability of actual prices customers are willing to pay.

In lean management accounting, understanding a value stream hurdle rate is a useful and simple tool to use to calculate a desired price. Hurdle rates are commonly used in investment analysis, such as determining whether to invest in a company or in a project. A hurdle rate is calculated to understand the minimum acceptable rate of return expected to be received on an investment. In lean decision making, a value stream hurdle rate can be used to calculate a desired price to charge to earn a desired profit.

Calculating the actual profitability in pricing and quoting is done by projecting a future state box score. A future state box score will consider the impact of both price and volume on overall value stream performance over the time frame of the decision. Let's now look at how one company uses these hurdle rates and box scores to provide quotes and analyze profitability.

Value Stream Income Statement Projection	Maintenance	% sales	
Sales	2,800,000		
Variable costs	1,204,000		
Contribution margin	1,596,000	57.00%	◁ Hurdle Rate
Fixed costs	616,000	22.00%	
Operating profit	980,000	35.00%	

FIGURE 8.7
Midwest Maintenance Hurdle Rate Calculation

Midwest Service Company is a regional truck service repair company that provides maintenance and repair services to companies that have truck fleets. Midwest has two value streams:

- Maintenance – which focuses on performing routine, preventative tasks such as oil changes, fluid top-ups and basic inspections.
- Major repair – which performs all repair services for customers.

A new customer approached the sales team and requested a quote to perform routine preventative maintenance for their fleet of 500 trucks. The sales team has a strong desire to acquire the business of this new customer in the maintenance value stream because they have also indicated that they are considering outsourcing their repair work in the next year.

Midwest's planning process produces an updated 12-month financial forecast each quarter for both value streams. From these updated forecasts, the accounting team calculates a value stream contribution margin hurdle rate, which is illustrated in Figure 8.7. The maintenance value stream's 57% hurdle rate is the sum of the operating profit percentage of sales plus the fixed cost percentage of sales.

The sales team uses this hurdle rate to prepare quotes as shown in Figure 8.8. To prepare this quote, the sales team uses estimated variable costs per truck of $17.00 based on the maintenance services the customer desires. The sales team calculates a quoted price of $39.53 using this formula:

Quoted price = variable costs per unit / (1- contribution margin
hurdle rate)

Variable cost per truck	• $17.00
Quote price:	• ($17.00 / .43) = $39.53
Customer RFQ:	• 500 trucks per month at $38.00
Questions	• Would you accept $38.00? • Is $38.00 still profitable? • Under what conditions?

FIGURE 8.8
Calculate a Quote Price

After receiving the quote, the customer tells the sales department it would like to pay only $38.00 per truck. This means the salesperson, the value stream manager and the value stream accountant must meet to calculate a future state box score to determine the impact on value stream profitability of accepting a price of $38.00 per truck.

The first step for the team is to calculate the impact the 500 trucks per month has on value stream capacity and the profitability, which is summarized in column B of Figure 8.9. At a price of $38.00 per truck the incremental contribution margin of 55.26% is slightly better than the current contribution margin of 52.78%, but there is not enough capacity to meet this demand, which is indicated by the available capacity of -1%.

The next step is for the team to model options for increasing capacity. It creates two future state box scores for two options: hiring more people (column C) and making improvements (column D).

The team concludes that accepting the customer's price of $38.00 per truck and hiring more people is not a good financial decision because it would decrease the return on sales from 29.63% to 27.48%, as well as decreasing productivity.

The value stream manager prefers making improvements to create the capacity because it generates an additional $15,000 of operating profit a month, decreases non-productive capacity and has a positive impact on performance. The salesperson also explains that they believe the good performance in the maintenance value stream will favor Midwest's acquisition of the repair services in the future.

Lean Performance Measurements	A Current State	B Opportunity	C Future State - Hire People	D Future State - Improvement
Productivity	$ 14,625		$ 13,243	$ 15,892
On-time delivery	81%		90%	90%
Quality	20%		20%	15%
Average cost per unit	$ 10.42		$ 10.91	$ 9.45
Lead time	8.21		7.44	7.44
Capacity				
Number of units produced	4875	500	5375	5375
Productive capacity	36%	41%	34%	41%
Non-productive capacity	52%	55%	50%	41%
Improvement capacity	5%	5%	5%	5%
Available capacity	7%	-1%	11%	13%
Value Stream Income Statement				
Revenue	219,375	19,000	238,375	238,375
Material	103,594	8,500	114,219	107,500
Contribution margin	115,781	10,500	124,156	130,875
	52.78%	55.26%	52.08%	54.90%
Value Stream Costs				
Labor - Regular	36,000		43,200	36,000
Labor - Overtime	3,375		4,050	3,375
Depreciation	6,400		6,400	6,400
Repairs & Maintenance	1,000		1,000	1,000
Other	4,000		4,000	4,000
Total value stream costs	50,775		58,650	50,775
Value stream profit	65,006		65,506	80,100
Return on sales	29.63%		27.48%	33.60%

FIGURE 8.9
Future State Box Scores

LEAN COST MANAGEMENT DECISIONS

Lean management accounting focuses on understanding the drivers, or root causes, of costs and applying PDCA to reduce costs over time. It's best to think of lean cost management as an integrated system embedded in a lean company, as opposed to something accounting does. It's based on principles, practices and tools which have been explained throughout this book and will be summarized again here.

- Economics of lean (Chapter 3) – continuous improvement creates capacity and how the freed-up capacity is utilized determines the financial impact. Over time, lean will reduce costs in two ways:
  - Actual cost savings will be realized because improvement activities reduce wastes that have specific costs, such as reducing scrap by improving quality.
  - The capacity created through improvement activities can be utilized to avoid future cost increases. A simple example is not having to hire additional employees to meet an increase in demand.

- Proper categorization of costs (Chapter 6) – costs are categorized based on how each cost actually behaves:
  - Variable costs – costs that vary in direct proportion to changes in short-term sales volume.
  - Fixed costs – costs that do not change in direct proportion to changes in short-term sales volume and are influenced by management decisions.
- Box score as an analytical tool (Figure 8.1) – the box score creates visibility and insight into the actual cause–effect relationships between lean operating performance and financial performance. Analyzing the incremental change between a current state box score and a future state box score will inform decision makers of the complete picture of any analysis and improve the quality of decision making.

Let's now look at some examples of how companies use box scores to manage their costs.

Labor Cost Management

Strategic Tax Services, LLC (STS) is a local accounting firm that performs audits and prepares tax returns, which are the two value streams of the company. The tax value stream has a staff of 20 and they prepare and file 1,000 tax returns a year. At the conclusion of this year's tax filing season the team met to review its performance using their value stream box score illustrated in Figure 8.10.

Janet, the tax partner, explained there were many opportunities for improvement for next tax season because 59% of the team's capacity (Figure 8.1, column A) was being used on non-productive activities such as fixing defects, checking and reviewing, set ups and other administrative activities. In the meeting she also announced that three employees, Mike, Jo Ling and Armando, will be retiring after next tax season.

Janet told the tax team the firm's managing partner wants to improve the profitability of the tax value stream by lowering labor cost as a percentage of sales from 45% to no greater than 40%. Using an adjusted current state box score (Figure 8.1, column B), Janet explained this target can be achieved after the three employees retire: labor cost will be 38% of sales, but there will not be enough capacity to prepare and file the 1,000 tax returns.

	A			B			C		
	Current State			Current State 3 staff leave			Future State with improvements		
Performance Measurements									
Productivity	$ 25,000			$ 29,412			$ 29,412		
Delivery	80%			80%			85%		
Average Set Up Time (minutes)	20			20			10		
Cost per Return	$ 289			$ 255			$ 255		
Quality (Defect Rate)	30%			30%			15%		
Average Overtime Hours per Day	5			5			2.5		
Average Processing Time (hours)	82			82			72		
Capacity									
Productive	42%			49%			59%		
Nonproductive	59%			64%			37%		
Available	-1%			-13%			4%		
Income Statement									
Revenue	500,000			500,000			500,000		
Materials	-			-			-		
Contribution Margin	500,000			500,000			500,000		
Value Stream Costs									
Labor	224,000	45%		190,400	38%		190,400	38%	
Operating	55,000			55,000			55,000		
Other	10,000			10,000			10,000		
Total Costs	289,000			255,400			255,400		
Value Stream Operating Profit	211,000			244,600			244,600		
Return on Sales	42.2%			48.9%			48.9%		

FIGURE 8.10
Tax Value Stream Box Scores

Janet further explained the managing partner has seen this box score and is challenging the tax value stream team to create enough capacity, so the firm does not have to replace the three retiring employees. Additionally, the managing partner wants to reduce the overburden on the value stream and reduce the average overtime hours from 5 per day to 2.5 per day.

The team scheduled a two-day improvement event to develop improvement activities that could be implemented throughout the next tax season. The first step of the event was to identify the specific non-productive activities:

Non-Productive Activity	Minutes	Percentage
Set up	28,000	16%
Defects	51,000	30%
Checking & reviewing	53,000	31%
Other	38,000	23%
Total	170,000	100%

Using the "5-Why" method of identifying root causes, the team identified the primary root cause of each type of non-productive activity and identified solutions to eliminate each root cause:

Category	Root Cause	Solution
Set up	Searching for information	5-S paper and electronic information
Defects	Clients deliver information in multiple formats	Initial face-to-face client meeting to review information
Checking & reviewing	4 rounds of review per return	Maximum 2 reviews per return

Based on these solutions, the team calculated a future state box score (Figure 8.10, column C) with the updated capacity numbers, and it clearly shows that these improvements will create enough capacity to process the tax returns without having to replace the retired employees.

What the tax value stream team learned is that labor cost represents how much is being paid for a fixed amount of capacity. In lean management accounting, managing labor cost is about developing a deep understanding of how employees spend their time, which can be either on value added, or non-value added activities. The box score capacity measurements make this information visible. The tax value stream team was able to use the detailed non-value added activity information to develop improvements to reduce non-productive capacity, increase available capacity, and control its labor cost.

In professional service companies that invoice customers based on billable hours, the same approach to labor cost management can be used at a job, project or contract level. This is possible because the same relationships between labor costs and activities apply. Understanding the root causes of actual billable hours for a job is about understanding the non-value added activities consuming the time of the employees through the use of lean performance measurements and daily lean management practices, rather than traditional time-tracking activities.

Machine Cost Management

In some companies, machines provide capacity to perform value added activities, and the box scores are effective for managing these costs. Waste and unavailability drive machine costs so it is important to measure these aspects of machine performance in box scores:

- Scrap or first time through rate.
- Downtime rate.
- Changeover times.

Improvement activities focusing on reducing the forms of waste listed above will ultimately manage machine costs such as replacement part expense, outside maintenance costs and overtime of operators and maintenance employees. If a lack of machine capacity has forced a company to outsource some production, then this cost can also be reduced by creating machine capacity to in-source previously outsourced work.

Material Cost Management

In some industries, material costs are a primary variable cost, such as:

- Parts and supplies in repair companies.
- Food in restaurants.
- Medical supplies and drugs in healthcare.
- Raw materials and inventory in manufacturing.

In lean management accounting, material cost management practices focus primarily on managing the quantity of material consumed rather than the price. The quantity of material consumed is a function of:

- Flow – the faster materials move through a value stream, the faster they are converted into revenue and cash.
- Scrap – consumes material and time and is pure waste.
- Inventory – consumes cash and time, reduces flow and is pure waste.

In value streams which use materials, controlling material cost is about having relevant lean performance measurements to measure the three factors listed above that influence the quantity of material consumed. Improvement activities to reduce scrap and inventory will have a direct impact on reducing actual material cost and, in the case of inventory, increase cash. The financial impact of improvement activities that improve flow will not reduce cost but can drive sales growth and increase cash by reducing the cash conversion cycle.

Material Price

In lean management accounting, price reduction has less of an impact on total material cost than quantity because lean companies usually don't seek out the lowest priced suppliers. This is because they recognize price is a function of value. Lean supply chain practices seek suppliers who deliver the highest value in terms of quality, delivery and lead time, at the lowest price.

WRAP UP: LEAN DECISION MAKING

When I work with companies, I always tell them that building a box score is the easy part of a lean management accounting transformation! Using the box score in decision making is the difficult part of the transformation. It's difficult because it requires decision makers to change thinking habits using new numbers they are not yet familiar with.

Thinking habits will change with practice over time. But just like learning anything new, decision makers may need mentoring and coaching while using box scores for decision making. This is where the role of accounting as financial coaches, as explained in Chapter 2, comes into play. Providing the necessary coaching support for lean decision making will accelerate the learning process of decision makers and improve the quality of decision making.

9

Dealing with Standard Costing: Simplifying Standard Setting

INTRODUCTION

Standard costing systems are deeply embedded in companies that use them, as illustrated in Figure 9.1. In most cases, standard costing systems are a component of a company's Enterprise Resource Planning (ERP system), which is usually a significant investment for a company. The information produced by a standard costing system is used in management accounting to measure performance and analyze profitability. In financial accounting, standard costing values inventory for financial reporting. A standard costing system also goes a long way to defining the role of accounting and accountants in using and maintaining the system.

The problem with standard costing systems is that they do not work well in lean companies because they were designed to support mass production manufacturing. Standard costing works well in mass production manufacturing, because one of mass production manufacturing's operating elements is stability and repetition. Frederick Winslow Taylor's *Principles of Scientific Management* (1911), which forms the foundation for mass production, stressed optimizing and simplifying tasks by using time studies. People are assigned specific tasks, which are designed to take a specific amount of time. Actual times are measured against standard times to measure operating efficiency.

Because inventories in mass production companies were quite large, specific identification of inventory costs became too difficult. That led to the development of standard costing systems to perform inventory valuation. Standard costing systems use the time-study information to calculate a standard product cost, which is used to value inventory and cost of

FIGURE 9.1
Standard Costing Systems

goods sold. This naturally led to accounting using production variances to measure the efficiency of operations and product costs for profitability analysis.

As a Lean CFO, if your lean company uses a standard costing system it is inevitable that you, and your company, will have to "deal" with standard costing because it contains a great deal of waste, as summarized in Figure 9.2. Poor quality is the primary source of waste in standard costing systems in lean companies because the information it produces is no longer relevant or reliable to decision makers. This waste is eliminated by developing a lean management accounting system.

Because a lean management accounting system is "standard cost free," it means the remaining use of a standard costing system is to value inventory for financial reporting purposes, which still requires setting standards and reporting transactions. This creates an opportunity to apply continuous improvement to your standard costing system to eliminate waste

Defects	• Information is not relevant or reliable to users
Overproduction	• Information is produced and not used
Waiting	• Long feedback loops prevent root cause analysis
Neglect of talent	• Activities beneath the talent level of users
Transportation	• Handoffs of information between systems and people
Inventory	• Annual setting of standards & rates
Motion	• Unnecessary searching for information
Excess processing	• Detailed transaction reporting

FIGURE 9.2
Standard Costing System Waste

in standard setting and production reporting processes. Another improvement opportunity is to "turn off" standard costing for inventory valuation purposes and replace it with a lean inventory valuation methodology.

This chapter, and the next two, are written to explain the sequence of possible improvements you can make to your company's standard costing system, based on the actual improvements made in companies I have worked with. This chapter will explain how to simplify standard setting; Chapter 10 will explain how to eliminate unnecessary ERP transactions; and Chapter 11 will explain how lean inventory valuation methods can be used to replace standard costing.

STANDARDS ARE STATIC, LEAN IS DYNAMIC

As a Lean CFO, you must recognize early in your company's lean transformation that lean practices will wreak havoc on standard setting. Setting standards for costing purposes requires making many static assumptions about the data that are used to calculate standard costs. Lean practices are dynamic because they are all about changing and improving production processes, the physical layout, and having flexibility with people and machines.

The impact of lean on a standard costing system will be more fluctuation of absorption and variances, which will be even more difficult to explain than before becoming lean. The reason this will occur is that the rate of change in lean operations makes the assumptions used in standard setting invalid, and keeping all the assumptions up to date is an impossible task.

It's best to be proactive and begin simplifying standard setting at the beginning of a lean transformation. Being proactive in this will prevent a lot of unnecessary work in the future, like trying to answer, "What's going on with standards or variances?" This needs to be looked at as a series of problems to be solved based on exactly how the detailed input is used to set standards.

Simplifying standard setting is based on understanding how your ERP system uses various pieces of data and information to calculate standard costs. Fortunately, all ERP systems do this pretty much the same way, although the terminology each ERP system uses may be different. The configuration of routers, bills of material, material costs, labor, and overhead rates determines the complexity of a standard costing system. Let's now look at how to improve setting these standards, beginning with information used to calculate material costs.

SIMPLIFYING MATERIAL STANDARD SETTING

Material cost is calculated from the bills of material. The components of bills of material are used by a standard costing system to do some basic math – multiply the quantity of each line item by its standard cost and total these costs to get the standard material cost of a product.

Lean practices, primarily around improving the flow of materials, create improvement opportunities to simplify the components of bills of material used to set material standard costs, which are summarized in Figure 9.3. Let's look at each opportunity in detail.

Reducing the Number of Bills of Material

A bill of material must be created for any product that gets recorded as completed production in an ERP system – all finished goods, as well as any sub-assemblies that get recorded into stock. In traditional manufacturing,

	Traditional drivers of complexity	Lean drivers of simplicity
Number of bills of material	Each item reported as sub-assemblies and finished goods	BOMs based on finished goods only
Number of parts and line items	MRP, purchasing and "inventory control" by ERP	Pull systems and visual control
Quantity per assembly	Costing, purchasing and "inventory control" by ERP	Actual quantity based on product design
Material cost	Standard costing and variance analysis	Average cost or last price paid

FIGURE 9.3
Simplifying Bills of Materials

sub-assemblies are typically produced independently of the finished good that they are part of, so they require their own bills of material. The bill of material for the finished goods will have on it all sub-assemblies taken from stock, as well as other raw materials consumed.

Single piece flow and pull systems may eliminate the need for sub-assemblies to be stocked as inventory, because their production is coordinated based on the production of the finished goods rather than being independently produced. This means sub-assemblies don't have to be reported as completed production and thus do not need separate bills of material. The components of the sub-assemblies can be added to the bills of material of their respective finished good products. An improvement objective would be for the number of bills of material to match the number of finished goods that a company produces.

It is also possible to further reduce the number of bills of material based on ERP system features, especially in the case of custom products. In traditional manufacturing, producing custom products has an exponential effect on the number of bills of material because each unique part number must have a bill of material.

Some ERP systems have one-time "configurable" bills of material, which build a unique bill of material for a customized product as the material is consumed during production. Another ERP system feature is allowing the substitution of parts on existing bills of material to create a "new" bill of material for a new part. In both cases, it's possible to use system features and have even fewer bills of material to build and maintain.

Reducing the Number of Part Line Items

Traditional manufacturing companies like to list every possible item, no matter how large or small, on bills of material. The reasons for this are:

- To generate variances such as material usage for performance measurement.
- For system-based inventory control to be able to look "in the system" at quantities on hand.
- For purchasing purposes so material requirements planning modules (MRP) can produce purchase orders.

In a lean company, the pull systems and visual management practices in place on the shop floor and with suppliers will regulate the quantity of material purchased and used, eliminating the need for system control. Kanban signals from operations to purchasing and suppliers are used, eliminating the need for MRP to signal when to purchase. Point-of-use inventory in value streams manages the usage of materials, including allowable substitutions, eliminating the need for material usage variances.

Items on bills of material can be further simplified by eliminating small parts, such as screws, or difficult-to-measure ingredients. Treat these items as shop supplies and incorporate kanban signals for reordering.

Improving Quantity per Assembly

Every item listed on a bill of material must have a quantity used. The actual quantity used for every part is typically determined in the product development process. However, because of the same reasons mentioned in the previous section – generation of variances and MRP-based purchasing – the actual quantity per assembly on the bill may be different.

For example, should the quantity per assembly include a yield rate, which is the scrap rate? If a yield rate is included, what should the yield rate be and how do we know it is consistent? Even more difficult are "parts" which are more like consumable supplies, such as paints and powders. The quantity used is often difficult to measure (e.g., "Who really knows exactly how much paint is used to coat a product?")

Improvement opportunities can focus on the goal of quantity per assembly being based on the actual quantity of a part needed to produce the product based on engineering specifications. The pull systems and visual management practices in operations will regulate the quantity of material purchased and used, eliminating the need for system control and MRP purchasing.

The lean performance measurement of quality is used to analyze scrap and other quality issues, identify root causes, and focus improvement efforts. When these lean practices are in place, quantity per assembly can be adjusted to actual quantity based on the design specifications.

Improving Material Cost

Traditional manufacturing companies spend a great deal of time determining the "standard" material cost to enter for each purchased part. The primary reason is to use purchase price variance (PPV) and material usage variance as performance measurements.

Some companies keep it simple: set the standard cost based on the price the supplier charges. Other companies try to get creative by entering the price they would like to pay, so that the effectiveness of the purchasing department, or suppliers, can be measured using PPV. In some cases, determining the purchase price is difficult. One example is commodity prices, which fluctuate frequently. In other cases, suppliers may change prices without warning. Lean companies recognize that PPV and material usage variance are meaningless measures.

Lean organizations usually don't seek out the lowest-price suppliers because they understand price is a function of value. Lean organizations want more out of their suppliers than the lowest price, they want their suppliers to be partners in improving material flow. Lean organizations seek suppliers who deliver the highest value in terms of quality, delivery, and lead time, *at the lowest price.* In many lean organizations, supplier certification programs are present where suppliers must continually meet agreed-upon performance requirements.

Improvement efforts should focus on moving away from determining a standard cost set annually to either average cost or last price paid. In many ERP systems, this is a system configuration setting that can be changed.

Improving material cost standard setting is best approached as a cross-functional series of improvements with the stakeholders in bills of material included – accounting, engineering, operations, and purchasing. By using the PDCA approach to improving material standard

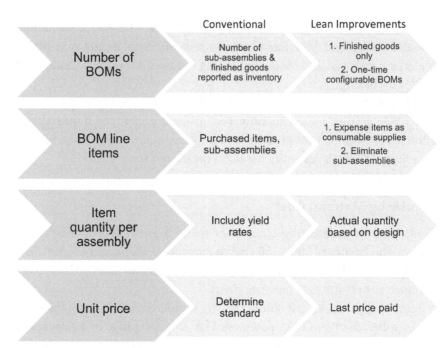

	Conventional	Lean Improvements
Number of BOMs	Number of sub-assemblies & finished goods reported as inventory	1. Finished goods only 2. One-time configurable BOMs
BOM line items	Purchased items, sub-assemblies	1. Expense items as consumable supplies 2. Eliminate sub-assemblies
Item quantity per assembly	Include yield rates	Actual quantity based on design
Unit price	Determine standard	Last price paid

FIGURE 9.4
Improving Bills of Material

setting, it's probable that every stakeholder will see the benefits of simplifying material cost standard setting, such as reducing the amount of nonproductive time that goes into maintaining bills of material. Figure 9.4 summarizes some improvement opportunities I have seen companies use in bills of material.

SIMPLIFYING LABOR AND OVERHEAD STANDARD SETTING

The source data to calculate labor and overhead costs are the labor and overhead rates and run rates for each step in a routing on a work order. This information, summarized in Figure 9.5, is somewhat subjective and must be estimated. The drivers of waste in labor and overhead rate standard setting are based on the conventional uses of standard costs:

- "Accurate" product costs to analyze profitability.
- Detailed reporting of sources of variances.
- Maximize overhead absorption.

Another aspect of complexity and waste in labor and overhead standard setting is configuring ERP systems to calculate the detailed rates. If you think of an ERP system as a very expensive calculator, it must be configured to the level of desired detail to do the calculations of product costs and measure variances at each possible production step. Let's review the complexity in ERP configuration first, before moving on to improvement approaches.

The first step is to identify all possible production steps in the factory that must be configured in the ERP system. These are typically called work centers or production steps in ERP systems. Accounting must develop labor and overhead rates for each work center as follows:

- Standard labor rate = labor cost / estimated labor hours
- Standard overhead rate = overhead costs / estimated labor hours or dollars

Some of these costs are easy to identify, such as how many people work in a work center. Overhead costs for each work center are more difficult to specifically identify. The conventional approach for overhead costs is to develop complex allocation schemes to assign as many costs as possible, so that the ERP system can create an "accurate" product cost.

	Traditional drivers of complexity	Lean drivers of simplicity
Number of rates	Detailed product costing by work center	Value stream cost analysis
Run rates	Detailed rates designed to maximize absorption	Simple average
Number of work centers & router steps	ERP production control; detailed product costing; variance analysis	Pull systems reduce the number of both
Number of routers	Each item reported as sub-assemblies and finished goods	Routers based on finished goods only

FIGURE 9.5
Simplifying Labor and Overhead Rates

The denominator in the standard labor rate calculation, estimated labor hours, is very much a guess. There are many factors that will drive estimating labor hours, such as estimating demand, product mix and production issues at each work center. Various analytical methods can be used to look at past trends, but past trends are not a predictor of the future.

Next step in configuring the ERP system is to create routers for each product. Routers are the specific sequence of work centers the product goes through in production. Each step on the router of a product must be given a run rate, which is the time it takes to complete the work in that process step. Determining the run rate is very similar to determining the quantity of each part on a bill of material. For products that are produced by machines the run rate may be easy to determine – the actual cycle time in the machine. However, this can be complicated by the desire to include set-up or changeover time as part of the run rate, which is driven by MRP planning and overhead absorption purposes.

For products that are assembled by employees, the run rate can be more of an estimate, due to a variety of issues. One simple example would be the case of a more experienced worker being able to assemble a product at a rate 20% faster than an inexperienced worker. What is the correct run rate to use? Run rates may also be set at the ideal run rate, to generate variances. Some companies also include set-up or changeover time to inflate run rates and increase absorption. Many factors can come into play in estimating labor run rates.

Routers become part of work orders or job orders in ERP systems. At a basic level, the purpose of work orders is to convert the raw material into finished goods in the ERP system. As production steps are completed, the work order will calculate standard labor and overhead costs, add these costs to the material cost and calculate the standard cost of the finished good.

If actual material and time are reported against work orders, it will also calculate an actual cost and variances. In Chapter 10, we will discuss transaction elimination as it relates to work orders.

Let's now look at improvement approaches to simplify labor and overhead rate setting.

Impact of Lean Practices on Routers and Rates

Creating flow in production is really re-designing processes based on lean practices. This means that current work centers will probably be combined, eliminated, or sequenced differently based on physical changes in operations. Continuous improvement can also have an impact on the cycle times to complete a production step, the number of people needed in a production step, as well as eliminating downtime and changeover time. This means that today's physical layout and work activities, which drive the ERP configuration and rate setting, will constantly be changing. This makes it very difficult to keep detailed work centers, routers and rates up to date.

Reduce Number of Labor and Overhead Rates

Box scores and lean performance measurements eliminate the need for detailed product costing and variance analysis. This create the opportunity to reduce the number of labor and overhead rates. Inventory still must be valued using the standard costing system, but the new objective is the total valuation of inventory rather than product-by-product. The goal would be to continually reduce labor and overhead rates and strive for one labor rate and one overhead rate for each location.

Simplify Run Rates

The need for highly engineered run rates to measure operating performance variances is replaced by lean performance measurements and visual lean operating practices. The need for "accurate" run rates to calculate an accurate product cost is also eliminated. Run rates for machines can be at the actual cycle time, without any set-up time included. Labor run rates can be a simple average, based on lean-focused time studies.

Reduce Number of Work Centers

Detailed work centers and routers on work orders are used to report actual to generate variances by production step. With lean operating practices, the need for variance analysis is eliminated. Daily lean management practices, as explained in Chapter 7, are used to control cell operations and identify gaps from standard. Pull systems regulate both production and inventory in a value stream. Every resource in the value stream knows through visual signals what needs to be worked on and when.

This creates the opportunity to reduce the number of work centers in the ERP system. Fewer work centers mean fewer labor and overhead rates. Fewer work centers also mean fewer production reporting steps on work orders. This opportunity is company specific and may even be value stream specific. Here are some general guidelines to consider.

- High volume production – if the total production time for products is minutes or a few days, it may be possible to have one work center for each product or product families that with the same production steps.
- Low volume production – if total production time is weeks, it would be best to consider any other uses of the work centers and reduce them to the minimal necessary for these other uses.

Strive for One Labor and One Overhead Rate

Figure 9.6 summarizes improvement opportunities in setting labor and overhead rates. Detailed labor rates, overhead rates and production

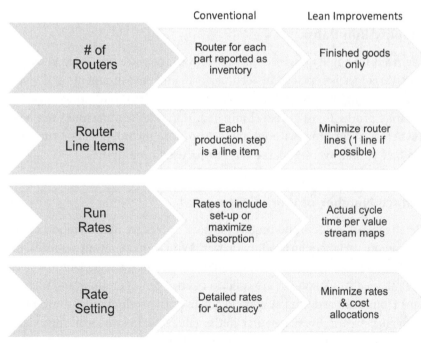

FIGURE 9.6
Improving Labor and Overhead Rates

reporting are used to achieve detailed product costs and variances for analytical purposes, which are not used in lean management accounting. For your company, develop an improvement approach that strives to continually reduce the number of rates towards a goal of one labor and overhead rate per location.

WRAP UP – SIMPLIFY STANDARD SETTING

Flat bills of material, a minimal number of work centers, one-step routers, and single plant-wide labor and overhead rates will greatly simplify your standard costing system, while still allowing you to use it to value inventory at a macro level. This work can begin early in your company's lean transformation. By simplifying standard costing, you will also be eliminating a tremendous amount of waste in your accounting processes, and you can reallocate this created capacity towards lean management accounting.

The next step in dealing with standard costing is to eliminate the waste of unnecessary production reporting transactions, which will be explained in Chapter 10.

10

Dealing with Standard Costing: Transaction Elimination

ERP AND THE CFO

Enterprise Resource Planning (ERP) systems are an integral part of every manufacturing company and also a very large investment in terms of cost, maintenance and support. Every employee, at some level, interacts with the ERP system, whether to process transactions, record information, read reports or use the information in decision making. The daily functioning of a company is totally dependent on an ERP system, which is exhibited in Figure 10.1.

As a CFO, you have a major stake in your company's ERP system. Your financial reports are produced from the general ledger maintained in the ERP system. The source of much of the accounting data comes from production transaction reporting. Revenue recognition is dependent on which products are made and shipped. Inventory value is based on properly recording material transactions. And in a product costing system, variances, absorption, and cost of goods sold are all based on transactions. Proper control of these transactions is essential to accurate and reliable financial statements.

In traditional manufacturing companies, accounting and operations usually agree on the need and uses of the ERP system. Traditional manufacturing operating practices use ERP to schedule and plan the execution of work, track inventory, and report operating performance. The transaction control gives both operations and finance the information they need for control and reporting.

This common ground between operations and accounting on ERP systems begins to diverge when lean is introduced into a company. One

DOI: 10.4324/9781003304098-10

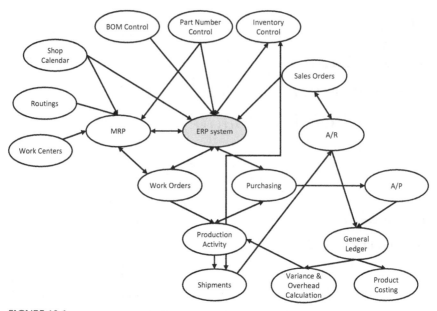

FIGURE 10.1
Typical ERP System Flowchart

way to look at this is it creates conflict, but another way to look at it is as an opportunity to eliminate waste in ERP transaction reporting. Let's compare the role of ERP in traditional and lean manufacturing.

TRADITIONAL MANUFACTURING AND ERP

ERP systems are designed to support traditional manufacturing management practices of "transactional control." Transactional control allows users to use the various tools of the system to plan, track and control production, inventory, purchasing and costs. ERP systems are designed to collect and report unlimited amounts of information based on how a company configures the set-up of the software. Figure 10.2 illustrates a typical level of detailed ERP transactional control in a traditional manufacturing environment. Another feature of ERP systems is the ability to summarize and report information to management to support top-down decision making.

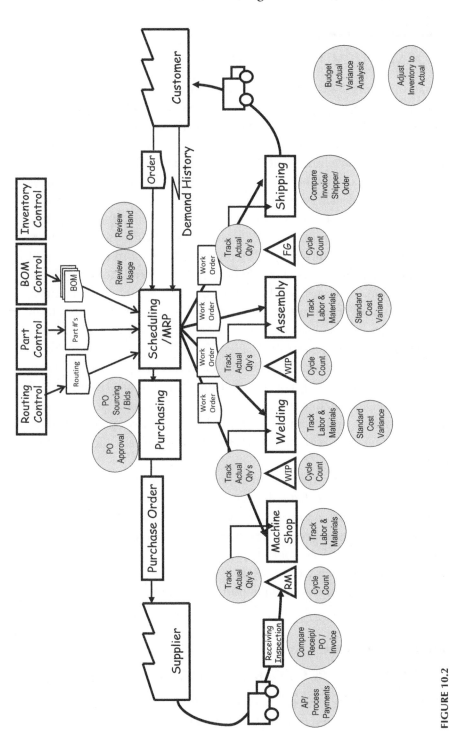

FIGURE 10.2
ERP Transactional Controls in Traditional Manufacturing

LEAN MANUFACTURING AND ERP

A lean operating system is a real-time execution system. It is proactively designed to flow actual (orders) as fast as possible through value streams. Flow is continually managed and maintained visually by the people in the value stream. What needs to be worked on can be seen, and interruptions to flow are made visible immediately and dealt with rapidly.

The various lean methods and practices to create flow are referred to as a pull system, and such systems virtually eliminate the need for ERP transactional control. For example, all material is visible and at the point of use in the value stream. Kanban levels in supermarkets are used to regulate production and limit inventory. The impact is to stabilize the amount of material in operations based on kanban levels and send clear signals for replenishment. What needs to be worked on next, and in what quantities, is always "visible" to everyone. The need to track material movement in great detail in order to "look into ERP" to find out where material is located is mitigated with these controls.

Figure 10.3 illustrates the typical visual controls in a pull system. These practices can totally control operations from the point material is received from suppliers through to when finished goods are shipped to customers. The deployment and maturity of these lean practices open up opportunities to reduce or eliminate what are now unnecessary ERP reporting transactions.

It's best to consider transaction elimination as a series of continuous improvement activities that will occur over time, based on the effectiveness of lean controls. As lean controls become effective, they replace the transactional controls. From a CFO viewpoint, it is important to develop an understanding of lean controls primarily by going to the Gemba and directly observing their effectiveness.

Now let's look at improvement opportunities in transaction elimination.

REDUCING WORK ORDER TRANSACTIONS

Work orders are like a Swiss army knife – one tool that performs multiple functions. Work orders are used to initiate production, track production,

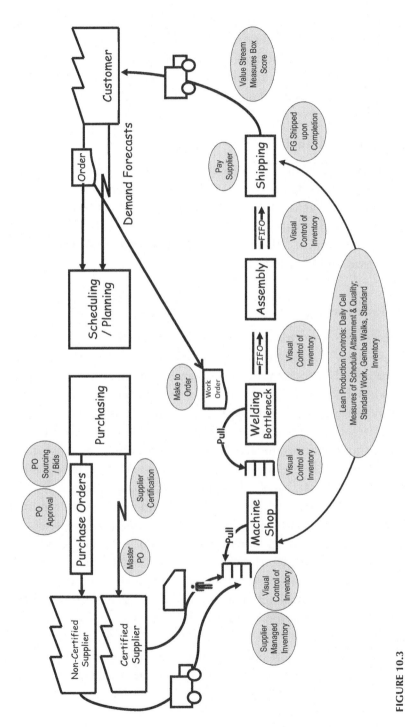

FIGURE 10.3
Lean Controls that replace ERP Transactional Controls

report completed production, report scrap, and report "actual," all of which require transactions. In addition, work orders may also provide work instructions or other technical information for operators.

Figure 10.3 summarizes improvement opportunities to reduce work order transactions, which will now be explained in detail.

Stop Reporting Actual

Actual material and labor are reported to work orders to generate variances for evaluating operating performance. The combination of lean performance measurements and daily lean management practices is used to identify gaps from standard in real time, which allows for both troubleshooting and just-do-it improvements. These practices eliminate the need for reporting actual material and labor to work orders.

Begin Backflushing

Every router step on a work order must be reported as completed so the work order can "move" the material from raw material through work-in-process to finished goods. Because actual is no longer being reported, the opportunity to introduce backflushing can reduce the number of router steps that must be reported as completed. Backflushing is best explained visually.

Figure 10.5 illustrates a work order with 10 production steps in its router. Without backflushing, each of the 10 steps must be reported as completed, as well as opening and closing the work order, for a total of 12 transactions. When backflushing is introduced, specific router steps can be selected as reporting steps and when these steps are reported the ERP system assumes the previous steps were also completed. In Figure 10.5, let's say router steps three, five and seven are selected as reporting steps. When step three is reported complete, the system will also record steps one and two as complete. And when the work order is closed, the system will automatically record steps eight through ten completed. In this example, backflushing has now reduced work order transactions by 58%!

Over time, as the flow of orders moves faster through a value stream, backflushing can be adjusted to further reduce the number of reporting steps, with a goal of two reporting steps – opening and closing the work order.

Improvement	Lean Control in Place
Stop reporting actual	Lean performance measurements and daily lean management
Backflushing	Lean performance measurements
Reduce router steps	Basic visual production controls
One-step router	Effective pull throughout production
Decrease number of work orders	Basic visual production controls, fewer sub-assemblies in stock

FIGURE 10.4
Reducing Work Order Transactions

Traditional Job Step Reporting – 12 transactions

FIGURE 10.5
Example of Backflushing

Backflushing – 5 transactions

Reduce Router Steps

The first two improvement opportunities eliminate the need for detailed routers on work orders. Basic visual controls throughout the value stream will regulate the work between cells and create initial improvements in flow, which further mitigates the need for detailed router steps. As pull systems provide more effective control, router steps on work orders can be reduced by having as few steps as possible on work orders. A goal to strive for would be one router step – produce the product! Fewer router steps mean fewer transactions reported.

Decrease Number of Work Orders

As mentioned in Chapter 9, a work order must exist for every item reported to stock, either as a finished good or sub-assembly. As flow is introduced into a value stream, one outcome may be that sub-assemblies are now produced in a make-to-order fashion rather than make-to-stock. If this is the case, these sub-assembly work orders can be eliminated, and the production steps may be combined into finished good work orders.

Another improvement opportunity to reduce the number of work orders is to align work orders to sales orders rather than aligning them to each production step. In traditional manufacturing, as illustrated in Figure 10.2, the MRP system may generate work orders for each step in the production process, which in this example means four work orders for every sales order. This is often done to maximize utilization of each resource. Figure 10.6 illustrates how aligning work orders with sales orders can reduce the number of work orders in this example from four per sales order to one.

In lean management accounting, the sole purpose of a work order is to convert the raw materials into finished goods, at standard cost, so products can be shipped to customers. The ERP system does all the calculations. As a Lean CFO, reducing work order transactions is a great opportunity to work with operations on continuous improvement, which will free up valuable time in both accounting, where transactions no longer have to be analyzed, and in operations, where transactions no longer need to be done.

WORK ORDERS AND LOT TRACEABILITY

Many companies, for warranty and liability reasons, need lot traceability in order to determine when a specific product was produced. Work orders do a very good job of maintaining this information. It's important to remember to apply lean thinking to lot traceability issues to determine the minimum information requirements and match transaction reporting to those needs.

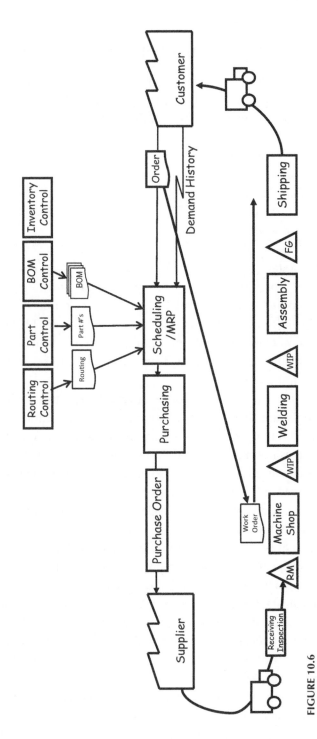

FIGURE 10.6
Align Work Orders with Sales Orders

REDUCING MATERIAL CONTROL TRANSACTIONS

ERP systems are configured to keep track of the quantity of materials on hand, as summarized in Figure 10.7. Inventory item quantity on hand is used in the system and by users to determine:

- Purchasing requirements
- Orders to ship
- Where to find items to use
- Where to store items
- The status of work-in-process

Keeping the system quantities accurate requires transactions to record every movement of material from receipt to each stocking location, through each production step to completion (using work orders), as well as transfers between locations. However, to make this happen, ERP systems also require the rate of transaction processing to keep up with the rate of material movement, as well as no inadvertent mistakes to be made when recording each transaction.

In reality, the rate of transaction processing rarely keeps up with the actual flow of materials and there are always inadvertent transaction reporting errors. The result is that oftentimes the quantity shown in the system at any point in time does not match the physical quantity, which can impact the types of decisions listed above. This also leads to the traditional solution of people involved in material management activities making inventory adjustment transactions, performing cycle counting or monthly physical inventories, all of which are wasteful.

Lean operational practices are specifically designed to manage the flow of materials visually and limit work-in-process inventory to kanban levels. Lean improvements in purchasing limit the number of raw materials. Make-to-order limits finished goods inventory. It is important for accounting and the Lean CFO to understand how these lean operational practices better control material and can replace the need for ERP-based transactional control.

The previous section of this chapter explained how lean practices can lead to fewer work order transactions. Now let's look at how lean practices can also eliminate the need for receiving transactions and material management transactions.

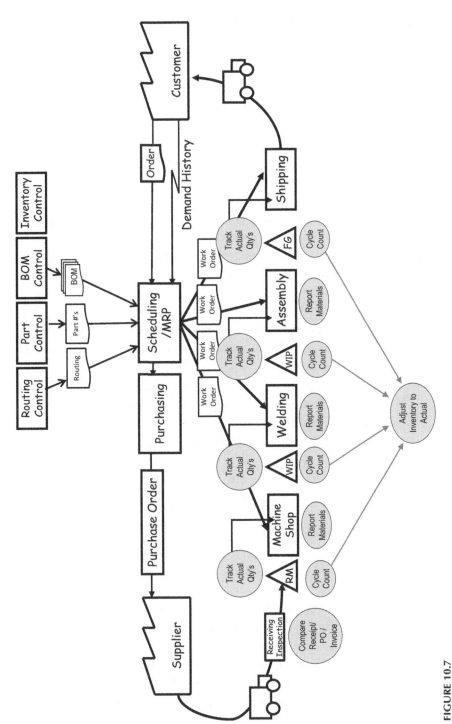

FIGURE 10.7
Material Control Transactions in Traditional Manufacturing

Reducing Receiving Inspection Transactions

The receipt of raw material into a company is a transaction that must occur. This makes the transaction non-value added, but necessary. A characteristic of non-value added but necessary activities is that waste may exist within the specific tasks which must be completed for the activity.

From a lean thinking viewpoint, wasteful activities in receiving inspection are checking and reviewing what suppliers send the company to make sure it is the right product and the right quantity. The following lean practices can be employed to eliminate these wasteful activities.

- Certified suppliers – Lean companies recognize that suppliers are essential to the success of improving flow and reducing lead times to customers. Lean companies develop supplier certification programs to improve overall supplier performance in on-time delivery, lead times and quality.
- Point-of-use delivery – Lean companies strive to reduce the unnecessary movement of materials, which is transportation waste. Suppliers deliver directly to point-of-use inventory locations, which are controlled by kanban levels.
- Vendor-managed inventory – Suppliers maintain standard stock levels of their product, which they own, at a company. The company pulls from the vendor managed inventory as needed, and suppliers periodically replenish stock to standard levels.

These lean practices improve the quality of the quantity received, and this can lead to the receiving transaction being based on:

- The purchase order quantity
- The amount pulled from vendor-managed inventory
- The kanban quantity replenished

These practices also create an opportunity in accounting to reduce the three-way match transactions. The three-way match is interesting – it's an established internal control practice in most manufacturing companies that does catch defects, but it does nothing to prevent defects. If your company does three-way match in accounts payable, think about the time and effort that is spent in accounting, purchasing and with suppliers in fixing the defects. Certified supplier programs, point-of-use delivery and vendor-managed inventory all can eliminate the three-way match transactions for suppliers that are part of these programs.

Reducing Inventory Adjustments and Cycle Counting Transactions

Lean operating practices such as kanban, supermarkets and pull systems are designed to control and limit the maximum amount of inventory in a value stream. These practices dramatically reduce the miscellaneous inventory adjustment transactions. Cycle counting inventory transactions may also be reduced because the kanban levels are the maximum inventory levels and the re-order points are the minimum levels. The actual inventory on hand is somewhere in between these two levels. Is it really necessary to do cycle counting if this is the case?

The maximum inventory levels developed in pull systems may also be able to be used in accounting to calculate work-in-process inventory levels, eliminating the need to use transactions to determine work-in-process percentage complete. If the difference between the maximum and minimum inventory levels in a pull system is immaterial to the valuation of inventory on the balance sheet, it's possible to simply use the maximum inventory quantities multiplied by a standard percentage complete to value work in process inventory.

PEOPLE SOLVE PROBLEMS

An ERP system cannot actively manage operational variability, it cannot identify root causes of waste and it cannot solve problems. Only people can perform these tasks.

WRAP UP: TRANSACTION ELIMINATION

Most ERP systems are configured based on traditional manufacturing practices to control through transaction reporting. In non-lean companies with high inventory, the allure of improved transaction control is very appealing because it's much easier for users to look on computer screens to understand how much material is on hand or the status of a work order.

The lean operating practices described in this chapter reduce the need for transaction control, *over time*. Eliminating transactions reduces the risk of entering defective information into ERP systems and it frees up the time of employees who enter and analyze transactions.

As a Lean CFO, collaborate with lean leadership and operations to develop a long-term transaction elimination plan. Identify the lean practices which have the potential to reduce transactions, identify the transactions, and develop objective measurements that determine "when" the lean practices are effective.

Now let's move on to what I consider "the pot of gold at the end of the rainbow" when it comes to dealing with standard costing systems, which is the ability to move away from standard costing for inventory valuation purposes.

11

Dealing with Standard Costing: Lean Inventory Valuation

INTRODUCTION

Inventory valuation is a necessary activity accounting must perform to maintain compliance with financial reporting standards. Standard costing is a method employed to value inventory, but as explained in the two previous chapters, it is a complex system with a great deal of detail, and it consumes a great deal of the time of many employees.

This chapter is going to explain what I consider one of the greatest improvement opportunities that exist in lean companies that use standard costing. It is the ability to "turn off standard costing" and use a more simplified, leaner method to value inventory for financial reporting purposes. The reason I call this a great opportunity is that lean inventory valuation means there is no longer the need to set standards; variances and absorption numbers no longer appear on financial statements; and all the time employees spend on these activities can be reallocated to more productive activities.

As a CFO I was able to do this, and throughout my career at BMA I have personally worked with companies, both public and private, that have been able to develop lean inventory valuation methods that meet financial reporting requirements.

As a Lean CFO, it is important to lead this effort because inventory valuation is a financial accounting requirement under Generally Accepted Accounting Principles (GAAP). Each company must create its own lean inventory valuation method that works best for itself. It's also important to learn what other companies have done, which will be explained in this

DOI: 10.4324/9781003304098-11

chapter. But before we look at lean inventory valuation methods, let's look at what GAAP says, and does not say, about inventory valuation.

GAAP AND INVENTORY VALUATION

Accounting standards are governed in the U.S. by Generally Accepted Accounting Principles, and by International Financial Reporting Standards (IFRS) throughout the rest of the world (for the sake of simplicity, I'm using use the acronym GAAP to mean both GAAP and IFRS). Although there are a few technical differences in these standards, it is important to know that both standards basically say the same thing about inventory valuation requirements.

The valuation of inventory and cost of goods sold is one of the most important issues for financial reporting because of it having a significant impact on the proper determination of income. GAAP states:

> Inventory has significance because revenues may be obtained from its sale. Normally such revenues arise in a continuous repetitive process or cycle of operations in which goods are acquired, created, and sold, and further goods are acquired for additional sales. Thus, inventory at any given date is the balance of costs applicable to goods on hand remaining after the matching of absorbed costs with concurrent revenues. In practice, this balance is determined by the process of pricing articles included in inventory.

What this means in layman's terms is that a portion of a company's expenses are moved from the income statement to the balance sheet. Expenses are reduced and this increases profits. Because inventory is usually one of the largest current assets on the balance sheet, it's easy to understand why inventory valuation is so important for proper financial reporting.

There are two issues related to inventory valuation – the value of inventory on the balance sheet and the determination of cost of goods sold.

GAAP states that inventory must be valued at cost, which is the same as all other assets on a balance sheet, and the components of inventory valuation are summarized in Figure 11.1. Cost is defined as the actual expenses incurred to get products in condition for sale, which are the actual cost

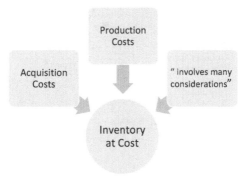

FIGURE 11.1
GAAP Inventory Valuation

of materials plus a portion of the actual costs of production. GAAP also recognizes the inherent complexity of inventory valuation: "it is understood to mean acquisition costs and production cost, and its determination involves many considerations."

Determining cost of goods sold is based on the matching principle which states that all expenses recognized in any reporting period should be the expenses *incurred* to generate the revenues recognized. Because cost of sales is often the largest expense on the income statement of a manufacturing company, it is significant to the proper determination of income. GAAP states this as follows: "A major objective of accounting for inventories is the proper determination of income through the process of matching appropriate costs against revenues."

The issues in a manufacturing company in determining cost of goods sold are related to the continuous nature of manufacturing, as summarized in Figure 11.2. Products produced in one period may not be sold until a subsequent period. The prices paid for purchased items may change. And finally, actual production costs change over time. This makes matching the specific, actual production costs to the revenue reported quite difficult.

GAAP recognizes that calculating the exact, specific cost of an item in inventory and cost of goods sold really cannot be done because of the timing issues of goods produced and sold, material costs changes and determining the exact manufacturing costs incurred for goods in inventory. GAAP states: "although the principles for the determination of inventory costs may be easily stated, their application, particularly to such inventory items

FIGURE 11.2
Difficulties in Inventory Valuation

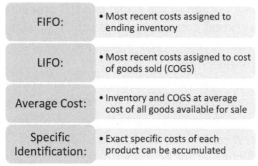

FIGURE 11.3
Cost Flow Assumptions

as work-in-process and finished goods, is difficult because of the variety of considerations in the allocation of costs and charges."

To overcome this problem, GAAP allows companies to use a cost flow assumption to value inventory and cost of goods sold in a consistent and systematic manner that best reflects income. Companies must use a consistent method over time, which means a company can't continually change its cost flow assumption to value inventory. If a company changes its cost flow assumption it is considered a change in accounting method and must be disclosed in audit reports. There are four cost flow assumptions that can be used: FIFO, LIFO, average cost, or specific identification, summarized in Figure 11.3.

In practice, cost of goods sold is really the difference between goods available for sale (beginning inventory + purchases) and ending inventory.

If the company's method of inventory valuation approximates cost, and is applied in a consistent manner, the company's financial statements are compliant with GAAP. Determining if inventory approximates cost and is applied in a consistent manner is usually done by a company's outside auditors.

It's important to note here that GAAP does not promulgate "standard costing" as an inventory valuation method. Standard costing is used to approximate actual cost, and if it does, auditors consider inventory and cost of goods sold to be properly valued. However, if audit tests conclude standards do not approximate cost, a company is required to adjust the value of inventory on its balance sheet, primarily by capitalizing variances, to follow GAAP.

LEAN INVENTORY VALUATION AND GAAP COMPLIANCE

One of the major impacts of lean is significant reductions in inventory over time. It's common to see annual inventory reductions of 25–50% as lean practices become established in manufacturing operations. When inventory levels reach the 30- to 60-day range, the financial risk of inaccurate inventory valuation decreases significantly, and the risk of material misstatement of profits is also reduced. Low inventories also create the opportunity for accounting to use simpler methods to value inventory and cost of goods sold for financial reporting purposes.

Lean inventory valuation methods use the cost flow assumption of *average cost*. With low inventories, it's easy to identify the actual material and production costs for the reporting period, especially when using a value stream income statement. Calculating the average cost is done at a higher level than individually costing each part, which is the basis for simplification of inventory valuation.

Migrating away from a typical standard costing system requires looking at material costs and "labor and overhead costs" (which we will now call production costs) separately to determine the best methods to use to get average cost. What we will look at now is approaches companies have used to put lean inventory valuation methods in place.

LEAN INVENTORY VALUATION OF MATERIAL

Calculating the material value of inventory using average cost is straight-forward and is dependent on the number of items purchased as raw material and their price stability.

Most companies usually have hundreds, or thousands, of items purchased as raw materials. In this case, simplification comes mostly from getting away from a unique standard cost for each part and moving to either an average cost for each part, or the last price paid. In many ERP systems, this is a configuration setting which can be changed.

It's most practical to continue to track material quantities and transactions in an ERP system, given the number of parts, mix and volume of transactions. The ERP system will continue to value each raw material part individually and the material components of inventory and cost of goods sold.

In the rare case where a company has only a few items that are purchased as raw materials, and low raw material inventory, additional simplification can be done by getting away from individual part costing and moving to an overall average cost. In this case, purchases can be expensed directly to the value stream income statement. At month-end, the value of material inventory can simply be calculated by the ratio of material on hand to total material purchased, at average cost. Ending material inventory can be recorded by using a journal entry.

In both examples, GAAP inventory valuation compliance is achieved because actual material costs are being used to calculate the average. The material costs which appear on a value stream income statement will represent the actual cost of materials consumed to generate the revenue recognized, which meets compliance with the matching principle.

LEAN INVENTORY VALUATION OF ACTUAL PRODUCTION COSTS

The ability to move away from capitalizing production costs on a product-by-product basis using standards creates the most opportunity to eliminate a tremendous amount of non-value added work and free up accounting resources to spend more time on serving its internal customers better.

Over the years I've worked with companies in developing lean inventory valuation methods for capitalizing production costs using either average costs or what I call historical margins. In both methods production costs are capitalized in total rather than product-by-product. The adjustment to inventory on the balance sheet is usually accomplished by a journal entry. This means labor and overhead rates can be set to zero, and inventory in the ERP system is at material cost only. Let's look at each method through some examples.

Average Production Costs

When developing a lean inventory valuation method for production costs, the decision to be made here is to determine the averaging factor, which is typically days of inventory or units of inventory, whichever is more readily available. The steps to calculate average production costs for any reporting period are:

1. Use total actual production costs from the value stream income statement.
2. Calculate average production costs using days of inventory or units of inventory.
3. Calculate ending inventory of capitalized production costs.
4. Make the adjusting journal entry.

The example in Figure 11.4 uses average production costs per day to calculate ending inventory. The value stream income statement shows $867,550 of actual production costs for 20 working days in the month, which means the average production costs per day are $43,828.

The ending inventory of production costs will be calculated based on the number of days of work-in-process and finished goods inventory. There are three days of work-in-process inventory, 50% complete, so the ending inventory of work-in-process is $65,741. Four days of finished goods inventory is valued at $175,310. The total ending inventory for production costs is the sum of these two numbers: $241,051.

The final step is to make the adjusting journal entry, which in this case is a $55,458 credit to inventory on the balance sheet and a debit for the same amount on the income statement.

Step 1: Total production costs	
Value Stream Income Statement	
Revenue	2,048,686
Materials	849,526
Contribution margin	1,199,160
Labor	655,405
Machines	116,550
Outside processing	53,731
Facilities	41,200
Other	9,664
Total production costs	876,550
Value stream operating profit	322,610
Step 2: Calculate average production costs	
Days in month	20
Production costs per day	$ 43,828

Step 3: Calculate ending inventory		
Inventory - Capitalized Production Costs	Days	Value
Raw material	10	$ -
Work in process (50% complete)	3	$ 65,741
Finished goods	4	$ 175,310
Ending inventory		$ 241,051
Step 4: Calculate adjusting journal entry		
Ending inventory		$ 241,051
Beginning inventory		$ 296,509
Adjustment		$ (55,458)

FIGURE 11.4
Production Costs per Day Method

The example in Figure 11.5, uses average production costs per unit to calculate ending inventory. The value stream income statement shows $876,550 of actual production costs and 22,861 units produced in the month, which means the average production cost per unit is $38.34.

The ending inventory of production costs will be calculated based on the number of units in work-in-process and finished goods inventory. There are 3,430 units of work-in-process inventory, 50% complete, so the ending inventory of work-in-process is $65,758. There are 4,573 units of finished goods, valued at $175,341. The total ending inventory for production costs is the sum of these two numbers: $241,098.

Step 1: Total production costs	
Value Stream Income Statement	
Revenue	2,048,686
Materials	849,526
Contribution margin	1,199,160
Labor	655,405
Machines	116,550
Outside processing	53,731
Facilities	41,200
Other	9,664
Total production costs	876,550
Value stream operating profit	322,610
Step 2: Calculate average production costs	
Units produced	22,861
Production costs per unit	$ 38.34

Step 3: Calculate ending inventory		
Inventory - Capitalized Production Costs	Units	Value
Raw material	11,430	$ -
Work in process (50% complete)	3,430	$ 65,758
Finished goods	4,573	$ 175,341
Ending inventory		$ 241,098
Step 4: Calculate adjusting journal entry		
Ending inventory		$ 241,098
Beginning inventory		$ 296,509
Adjustment		$ (55,411)

FIGURE 11.5
Production Costs per Unit Method

The final step is to make the adjusting journal entry, which in this case is a $55,411 credit to inventory on the balance sheet and a debit for the same amount on the income statement.

Historical Margin

Another method used by some companies is the historical margin method, where production costs are capitalized based on historical margins. These historical margins are reviewed annually or quarterly for possible adjustments. Let's look at how historical margin is used following Figure 11.6.

The company in Figure 11.6 has four value streams, each of which makes different products. The first step is to calculate labor and overhead as a percentage of material cost, all at "standard." As you can see in Figure 11.6, the products in each value stream have quite different components of material, labor and overhead.

Step 1: Calculate Labor and Overhead as a % of Material Cost

Inventory @ standard

Value Stream:	Stand	Calibration	Measurement	Optical Tooling	Total
Material	$ 345,472	$ 28,360	$ 82,901	$ 440,350	$ 897,083
Labor and Overhead	$ 152,008	$ 5,105	$ 73,782	$ 325,859	$ 556,754
Total	$ 497,480	$ 33,465	$ 156,683	$ 766,209	$ 1,453,837

Labor & OH as a % Material Cost	44%	18%	89%	74%

Step 2: Calculate Capitalized Production Costs

Ending Material Inventory

Value Stream:	Stand	Calibration	Measurement	Optical Tooling	Total
Material	$ 344,803	$ 124,784	$ 51,257	$ 476,671	$ 997,515

Labor & OH as a % Material Cost	44%	18%	89%	74%

Capitalized Production Costs	$ 151,714	$ 22,462	$ 45,619	$ 352,737	$ 572,531

Step 3: Make Adjusting Journal Entry

Ending inventory - production costs	$ 572,531
Beginning inventory - production costs	$ 623,744
Adjustment	$ (51,213)

FIGURE 11.6
Historical Margin Method

The next step, which does not appear in Figure 11.6, is to turn off labor and overhead rates in the ERP system by setting them to zero, then revalue inventory. This will make the system inventory material cost only. After the inventory revaluation, it is necessary to make an adjustment, using a journal entry to "recapitalize" the production costs that were included in inventory before setting the rates to zero.

Step 2 of Figure 11.6 illustrates the monthly calculation to perform. Each value stream's material cost is multiplied by its historical margin percentage to calculate the ending inventory of production costs, which totals $572,531. The final step (step 3 on Figure 11.6) is to make the adjusting journal entry which in this case is a $51,213 credit to inventory on the balance sheet and a corresponding debit on the income statement.

GETTING STARTED WITH LEAN INVENTORY VALUATION

Based on experience, it's best to pilot a few methods over time before making a final decision on the best method to use. It's also important to study the impact of moving to an average material cost and setting labor and overhead rates to zero on all the reports being generated by the ERP system. It's best to get the users of this information involved, such as internal audit, financial planning and analysis, to get input on the impact lean inventory valuation may have on how they use the reports. Finally, it's important to involve external auditors, because they will need to apply audit tests to the new inventory valuation methods and are always concerned with consistency in the audited financial statements.

After lean inventory valuation methods for material and capitalized production costs have been decided, a date needs to be set to transition from standard costing to lean inventory valuation. The end of an accounting period is best because changes need to be made in the ERP system. It's best to lock out users from performing transactions while changes are being made to standards.

THE BENEFITS OF LEAN INVENTORY VALUATION

Generally Accepted Accounting Principles for inventory valuation are more a set of broad principles rather than specified methodologies. These principles focus on requiring a consistent method of valuation over time that properly reflects the determination of income by selecting one of the permissible cost flow assumptions.

Lean inventory valuation methods use the average cost flow methodology and attempt to get the broadest average possible. Production costs are capitalized at a macro level via a journal entry. Material average costs can be at item level or at higher levels, depending on each company's specific circumstances.

The primary benefit of lean inventory valuation is the elimination of unnecessary work, which creates capacity (time) to re-allocate to other tasks. Much of accounting's work required in conventional inventory valuation is no longer required. The time and effort of setting detailed labor and overhead rates is eliminated. The time spent analyzing, explaining, and reconciling product cost information, variances and absorption is also eliminated. The average material cost is relatively simple to calculate and probably doesn't need to be updated too often unless the material is a commodity.

Lean inventory valuation can transform the traditional cost accounting function into a proactive team member of lean operations that provides relevant financial information and analysis to make sound business decisions that support a lean business strategy.

Lean inventory valuation also provides benefits to operations, through the elimination of production reporting transactions. Many transactions required under conventional inventory valuation methods are not required under lean inventory valuation, which frees up operations capacity that can be re-allocated to filling customer orders.

WRAP UP: LEAN INVENTORY VALUATION

It's up to the Lean CFO to lead this effort because inventory valuation is a financial accounting requirement under GAAP. Begin with the goal in mind – maintaining GAAP compliance in the leanest way possible. Each lean manufacturing company must create a lean inventory valuation methodology that works best for itself in complying with GAAP and being consistent over time.

Learn from others. Talk to other lean manufacturing companies that use lean inventory valuation. Learn how they made the transition, the issues they faced and the methods they use. There are many private and public lean companies that have transitioned from standard costing systems to lean inventory valuation systems.

If you use external auditors, bring them into the discussion early and have them partner with you as you transition to lean inventory valuation. They will provide very clear guidance on maintaining GAAP compliance.

Lean inventory valuation represents a great opportunity for the accounting departments of lean companies to eliminate unnecessary work, create capacity and use that capacity to provide value-added services to internal customers.

Appendix

The following tables are designed as checklists you can use to develop your company's lean management accounting transformation plan. These checklists can be used to determine your current state and multiple future states. I recommend using six-month cycles for each future state.

It's also best for a cross-functional team to complete these checklists – accounting, operations, lean leaders and senior leaders.

Please don't hesitate to contact me if you would like to discuss your plan: nkatko@maskell.com.

These checklists, as well as other "free things," are available to download at www.maskell.com.

Lean Management Accounting System
Transformation Checklist

Chapter 3: Lean is the Strategy

Statement	Not in place	Working on it	Fully in place	Next steps/ Action plan
Training & education on lean management accounting has been completed				
Lean management accounting has been integrated with the lean strategy				
A lean management accounting leader has been selected				
A lean management accounting transformation team has selected				
Value streams have been identified and defined				
Value stream shared resources have been identified				

Statement	Not in place	Working on it	Fully in place	Next steps/ Action plan
Employees have been assigned to value streams				
Machines & equipment have been assigned to value streams				
Value stream teams have been organized				
The reporting relationships and responsibilities between value stream teams and functional managers has been defined				
All employees clearly understand the matrixed value stream organization				
Value stream teams exist and have operational management over the value stream				
Economics of lean is understood by senior leaders, accounting and managers				

Chapter 4: Lean Performance Measurements

Statement	Not in place	Working on it	Fully in place	Next steps/ Action plan
The purpose of lean performance measurements, to reveal problems, is understood				
The Linkage Chart process is followed to develop all lean performance measurements				
Measures are relevant to lean and the process being measured				

Statement	Not in place	Working on it	Fully in place	Next steps/ Action plan
Teams own their measures: self-report and self-monitor				
Daily/cell lean performance measurements have been developed to measure:				
Schedule attainment				
Quality				
Cost				
Flow				
Safety				
Respect for people				
Daily lean performance measurements are piloted for 30 days				
Daily lean performance measurements are deployed in all value streams				
Daily lean performance measurements are deployed in all other business processes				
Weekly/value stream lean performance measurements have been developed to measure:				
Delivery				
Quality				
Lead time				
Flow				
Productivity				
Cost				
Safety				

Statement	Not in place	Working on it	Fully in place	Next steps/ Action plan
Respect for people				
Weekly lean performance measurements are piloted for 4 weeks				
Weekly lean performance measurements are deployed in all value streams				
Weekly lean performance measurements are deployed in all other business processes				
Monthly/company lean performance measurements have been developed to measure:				
Delivery				
Quality				
Lead time				
Flow				
Productivity				
Cost				
Safety				
Respect for people				
Monthly lean performance measurements are piloted for 3 months				
All non-lean performance measurements are no longer used				
For every lean performance measurement the following has been completed:				
Formula or equation				
Source of the data to calculate the measurement				

Statement	Not in place	Working on it	Fully in place	Next steps/ Action plan
Presentation format (number, graph, etc.)				
Who has responsibility for reporting the measure				
Who has responsibility for being accountable for the measure				

Chapter 5: Measuring Capacity

Statement	Not in place	Working on it	Fully in place	Next steps/ Action plan
Employees clearly understand the difference between value added and non-value added activities				
A data collection method - either by process step activities or position activities has been determined for all value streams				
The source of activity data collection information has been defined (value stream maps; direct observation, etc.)				
Standard work has been developed to calculate productive, non-productive and available capacity for all value streams				
Standard work has been developed to regularly update capacity calculations				
Capacity is measured all value streams				
Capacity is measured in all other business processes				

Chapter 6: Value Stream Income Statements

Statement	Not in place	Working on it	Fully in place	Next steps/ Action plan
Employees clearly understand the purpose of value stream income statements				
A cross-functional team is used to design and develop value stream income statements				
A simple, "Plain English" format has been designed				
The definition of variable and fixed costs is documented and understood				
Value stream income statements have been developed for all value streams, making visible:				
Sales or revenue				
Actual variable costs				
Contribution margin				
Actual, direct fixed costs				
If shared costs are shown, a simple method to assign these costs has been developed				
Value stream operating profit				
A company-wide income statement in a value stream format has been developed:				
Cost allocations are visibly segregated				
This income statement reconciles to the external reporting income statement				

Statement	Not in place	Working on it	Fully in place	Next steps/ Action plan
"Actual cost reports", using the value stream income statement design, have been developed for all business processes				

Chapter 7: Value Stream Management

Statement	Not in place	Working on it	Fully in place	Next steps/ Action plan
Planning the value stream - Strategy Deployment				
Senior leaders complete a company X-matrix				
Company has established long-term lean strategies (3-5 years)				
Senior leaders establish 3 - 5 annual objectives				
Senior leaders establish strategic, priority initiatives for the coming year				
Lean performance measurements are used to set targets and measure progress of all company initiatives				
Senior leaders rationally prioritize resources and time to achieve annual objectives				
Cascading X-matrices are used in value streams and functions				
Value stream box scores are integrated into value stream X-matrices				
The "catchball" process is used to negotiate and agree on initiatives: targets, resources and time				

Statement	Not in place	Working on it	Fully in place	Next steps/ Action plan
Value stream performance measurements are integrated into value stream X-matrices				
There is a monthly cross-functional review of strategy deployment and the following occurs:				
Sales forecast is updated				
Operational plans updated				
Financial forecast updated				
Improvement activities reviewed, updated and adjusted				
Improving the value stream				
Value stream box scores are integrated into value stream X-matrices				
Value stream/process maps are updated on a regular cycle				
Kaizen events are planned during value stream mapping events				
Value stream kaizen events are linked to annual value stream objectives				
Value stream box scores are used in mapping events				
Standard work for kaizen events exists, including:				
Box scores are used				
A pre-event planning checklist				
Standard, timed agendas exists for all events				
Event team members clear their schedules to participate in events				

Statement	Not in place	Working on it	Fully in place	Next steps/ Action plan
A set of kaizen "rules" reviewed before each event				
Documentation requirements for all kaizen events				
Report outs are conducted				
Each value stream conducts a weekly team meeting				
There is a standard agenda and time for the weekly value stream meeting				
Weekly value stream visual board layout is standardized and displays:				
Performance measurements				
Pareto or other root cause analysis				
Improvement activities & status				
Value stream box scores				
Value stream maps				
Short-term operational countermeasures are identified in the weekly meeting				
Root cause analysis is performed on new problems & issues				
There is a standard process to escalate problems & issues the team cannot address				
Trends of recurring problems and issues are used to plan continuous improvement events				
Each value stream team manages its own improvement activities				
Value stream improvement activities are scheduled as a part of "regular" work				

Statement	Not in place	Working on it	Fully in place	Next steps/ Action plan
Value stream improvement activities are conducted over a specific time frame with a due date				
Daily lean management				
Daily demand is planned and prioritized				
Daily demand is balanced to 80% of capacity				
Daily visual board layout is standardized and displays:				
daily demand and backlog				
status of work in process				
performance measurements from a linkage chart				
trends over time or control charts				
current problems & issues				
status of improvements				
Responsibility for updating visual boards has been defined				
A daily huddle is conducted around the visual board				
Attendance is required in the daily huddle				
There is a standard agenda and time for the daily huddle				
Short-term countermeasures are identified in the daily huddle				
Root cause analysis is performed on new problems & issues				
Just-do-it improvements are prioritized by the cell team				

Statement	Not in place	Working on it	Fully in place	Next steps/ Action plan
JDI improvement activities are conducted over a specific time frame with a due date				
There is a standard process to escalate problems & issues the team cannot address				
There is a daily managers' gemba walk of all daily boards & huddles				

Chapter 8: Lean Decision Making

Statement	Not in place	Working on it	Fully in place	Next steps/ Action Plan
Box scores have been developed for each value stream				
Box scores have been developed for all other business processes				
Box scores are updated regularly - weekly and/or monthly				
Standard costing information is not used in lean decision making				
Standardized work for box score decision making is documented:				
calculate current state and future state box scores				
calculate the total incremental change to a box score over the time frame of the decision				
economics of lean is considered in all decisions				
subject matter experts are part of decision making process				

Statement	Not in place	Working on it	Fully in place	Next steps/ Action Plan
PDCA process is used in decision making				
Box score decision making is used in these types of decisions:				
profitability of sales orders				
profitability new demand				
profitability of new products and services				
calculating capacity requirements to meet demand				
hiring decisions				
capital expenditures				
pricing and quoting				
make or buy				
supply chain/purchasing				
measuring impact of continuous improvement events				
value stream mapping				
budgeting, planning, forecasting				
sales, operations and financial planning activities				
senior leadership strategic decisions				
on-going cost analysis & management				
daily lean management decisions				
weekly value stream management decisions				

Chapters 9,10,11: Dealing with Standard Costing

Statement	Not in place	Working on it	Fully in place	Next steps/ Action Plan
Relationships between current management accounting system and standard costing are understood and documented				
Simplifying material standards				
Bills of material components and relationship to standard setting are understood				
Sub-assembly bills of material are reduced as flow improves				
ERP features to simplify custom bills of material are understood				
Low value items on bills of material are removed and treated as supplies				
Kanban has replaced MRP to determine purchasing requirements				
Item quantities are at actual and don't include yield rates				
Item cost is at average cost of last price paid				
Simplifying labor and overhead standards				
System calculations of using labor and overhead rates are understood and documented				
All reports and users of standard labor and overhead rate information have been identified				
The impact of simplifying labor and overhead standards has been studied and documented				
The number of work centers is continually reduced because of flow				

Statement	Not in place	Working on it	Fully in place	Next steps/ Action Plan
The number of router steps on work orders is continually reduced because of flow				
Router run rates are simplified to actual and no set-up is included				
Labor and overhead rates are continually reduced				
Transaction elimination				
A plan has been developed to study the impact of lean operating practices in value streams which includes transactions that can be eliminated when lean controls are effective:				
Certified suppliers				
Point of use inventory				
Vendor management inventory				
Kanban				
Supermarkets				
Visual controls of Flow				
Lean inventory valuation				
The impact of standard costs on reports is understood and documented				
Outside auditors and internal audit are part of the lean inventory valuation team				
Material cost is calculated as average cost per unit or last price paid				
Actual production costs can be calculated				

Statement	Not in place	Working on it	Fully in place	Next steps/ Action Plan
Averaging methods are studied				
Lean inventory valuation methods are piloted/run concurrently without impacting the ERP system				
Lean inventory valuation transition plan is developed				
lean inventory valuation is completed				
Labor and overhead costs are set to zero				

Index

Note: Entries in *italics* refer to figures; entries in **bold** refer to tables.